By CHRISTOPHER

The Craziest Thing You Ever Saw

The Salsa Project

Ten Tall Tales from West Africa

The Evidence-based Medical Mission

Move Over, Viola

Frontline Healthcare Hero

TEN TALL
TALES
FROM WEST
AFRICA

CHRISTOPHER
DAINTON

―――――――

*To my mom, who has been asking me for pictures
from Africa, and so I wrote this instead, which was
significantly more time consuming.*

*And Melody, for whom this is at least better
than a magnet.*

―――――――

"*The most that any one of us can seem to do is fashion something — an object or ourselves — and drop it into the confusion, make an offering of it, so to speak, to the life force.*"

ERNEST BECKER, THE DENIAL OF DEATH

CONTENTS

LETTERS
FROM AFRICA

MY FIRST ENCOUNTER WITH WEST AFRICA IS ABOARD THE connecting flight from Paris to Dakar.

Melody, my travel companion, is half a dozen rows in front, since we've agreed there is no need to add six more hours to the uninterrupted month we will be spending together. I should point out that there is nothing difficult about Melody, other than the indisputable fact that she is an extrovert and I am an introvert. It's like being a battery that charges while I am alone, and then slowly discharges in the presence of another person. Whether that battery will survive the next thirty-eight days is anyone's guess.

So instead of Melody, there will be a stranger in the seat neighbouring mine. I have already organized my seat pocket with my water bottle, mixed nuts, and Albert Camus novel when a large Senegalese man pulls up next to me wheeling his carry-on luggage. He immediately negotiates me out of my prized aisle seat by making an unambiguous declaration of terms (or perhaps, a thinly veiled threat):

"*Je sors frequemment.*"

It means he gets out frequently. I have no reason to doubt him. I concede immediately, shuffling my body into the cramped middle seat. Good Canadians are too polite to say no.

And with that, my flight companion henceforth becomes this heavyset African man, bald save for the white stubble that flecks his chin. He wears an elegant purple dashiki with a matching flat *taqiyya* cap, the outward trappings of his Islamic faith. He is not the only one in traditional dress aboard this plane. The many dashikis scattered among the rows fascinate me, because why travel, if not to be fascinated by the unknown?

But my companion's *particular* dashiki does not breathe well, and its fabric radiates a pungent odour that wafts over me whenever he raises his arm. He commandeers my armrest at will, at least when he isn't draping his arm over the seat in front of him. Everything about him is *big* and unapologetically so, from his enormous hands to his extravagant gestures. For six hours, he stares silently at the flight map. A tiny airplane creeps slowly across the screen, making its way from Paris to Dakar – the city that I presume to be his home.

I can't tell what he is thinking. Being human, and awake, I assume that his mind is processing some painful or pleasurable memory, perception, concept, or nascent plan, to which I am not privy. I can only experience him on his most superficial level, the one staring blankly at that pixelated icon. That bothers me.

What's more, that foreignness intimidates me. The idea of breaking this tension is terrifying. In the end, I don't speak to him and he doesn't speak to me. Even if I did, what would we even say?

MY EMAILS HOME WERE SIMPLE. THAT'S BECAUSE MY SENTI- ments prior to experiencing West Africa firsthand were coloured by prejudice and misconception. I don't apolo- gize for that, since ignorance is something better acknow- ledged and learned from than it is a defect of which to be ashamed. But I can divide my misconceptions into three main categories.

First, there was the fear, manifested in my need to ex- plain to anyone who asked that I would soon be traveling to my imminent death. I constructed a list of likely ways I could die: rabies, Ebola, malaria, political instability, kid- napping, cobra envenomation, violent crime, and African sleeping sickness. These are listed in no particular order.

That fear also relates to the unfortunate (or fortun- ate) timing of my trip, which coincided perfectly with an international crisis in which a Ukrainian passenger jet was accidentally shot out of the sky by the Iranian military. A tense time for the world, although in retrospect it would become substantially more tense. Suffice to say that my mother mainly wanted to know if we would be flying over Tehran on our way to West Africa.

Her anxiety meant that most of my emails were formulaic and focused disproportionately on damage control. They looked something like this:

> *Subject line: Safely in [insert country/city]*
> *Dear mom,*
> *Today, I did not die in Africa.*
> *Love,*
> *Christopher*

But West Africa is much safer than most people give it credit for. Cast aside the unflattering headlines. It's easy enough to forget that real people live here – their entire lives – without being crippled by agonizing spasms of panic and existential dread. Quite the opposite, in fact. Existential dread is a Western conceit. At the risk of stereotyping an entire continent, Africans live their lives *fully*.

SECOND, THERE WERE THE MOSQUITOES.

In retrospect, what I was *most* worried about were the mosquitoes. Just under a month before leaving, I assessed a patient in the Emergency Department who was worried she might have a fever. She explained that she had spent some time in Senegal and Niger several months ago on an extended business trip, and that she had returned home with malaria. I asked if she had taken her malarone (a daily preventative medicine) religiously, and if she had ever missed doses.

Yes to the first question, no to the second. But you must understand, she said, that West Africa is *very mosquito-y*. And that might well be true under certain circumstances. Unless you take the time to properly cover your body head to toe in potent neurotoxins.

That meant that during my travel preparations, I took the time to read obsessively about how to escape the ravages of malaria while in Africa. And like the protagonist of a Tolkien novel in a vast medieval library – poring over hundreds of moth-eaten volumes by candlelight – I eventually encountered the summary of an old experiment using DEET and permethrin. In the study, volunteers were enclosed in a box infested with mosquitoes. Unprotected, they were bitten between 1200 and 1400 times per hour. After being thoroughly sprayed with DEET, the active ingredient in most mosquito repellants, they were bitten only forty times per hour. When wearing permethrin-impreg-nated clothing, they were bitten twenty times per hour. But when outfitted with *both*, they sustained *zero* bites per hour. I only hope they were paid well for their time.

From there began a month-long quest to obtain this fabled permethrin – banned by Health Canada on account of its potential neurotoxicity but legal in the United States, where the risk of noticeable neurologic damage would be much lower. This was a quest which narrowly failed when a package dispatched from New York was seized in transit by Canadian customs, but which eventually succeeded when we found the motherlode in an unassuming pharmacy during our Paris layover.

THIRD, THERE WAS THE UNDENIABLE FACT THAT WEST AF-rica is a strange place for a traveler to go. Now that we have established that a person *could* go to West Africa, in theory, it still remains to be proven whether someone *should* go there. To this second question, I encountered only one reaction, one that was almost universal. An innocent (and mostly harmless) question about whether I would be volunteering, or perhaps even doing a medical mission.

It's a perfectly reasonable question when you consider that humanitarian volunteering remains one of the only reasons that a non-African would find himself unexpectedly in Africa. But there's an inherent narcissism in the assumption that, without ever having previously set foot on the continent, one's first instinct should be to disembark and then attempt to *save Africa*. Without knowing anything about the culture or the people, what right do I have to arrive and expect to practice medicine?

What's more, the idea of *saving Africa* reduces the continent to a caricature of itself – implies that its major contribution to the world, its renewable resource, is a people who exist only as receptacles of charity. Of course, that has never been true. But it reflects a lack of imagination that is all too common.

For example, I will admit with some shame that one of the first books I looked for in West Africa was a French translation of the classic Joseph Conrad novel *Heart of Darkness*. Knowing nothing of the book except that it was a classic and that it involved an ill-fated journey into the heart of the continent during the colonial era, it seemed to make the perfect 'look smart on public transportation' type of travel accessory. But you won't easily find it in any bookstore in West Africa. In fact, in 1975, the celebrated Nigerian author Chinua Achebe described Conrad's novel as "an offensive and deplorable book that de-humanised Africans". That doesn't automatically make it so, but it does suggest that it's not a book that I would want protruding from my backpack pocket.

But in many ways, Africa is also one of the world's few remaining *big adventures*, as unexplored culturally as geographically. You wouldn't know it looking at a map, but all of the enormity of Russia or Canada fits easily inside just the continent's northern half. On this trip, Melody and I set out from Dakar (Senegal) to Lomé (Togo). On a map, that distance appears miniscule. It looks like one could cross those nine West African borders by simply cruising along a coastal highway.

In reality, Dakar to Lomé amounts to a staggering 3459 km, the distance from Barcelona to Moscow. And nothing about travel in West Africa involves anything resembling cruising, nor does anything exist that resembles a coastal highway. The road trip also requires numerous visas issued by embassies in Ottawa and Washington, for countries with perpetual travel advisories and warnings. Honourable mention goes to the Côte D'Ivoire embassy website, with its fanciful multiplicity of colours and fonts, and its links to two separate visa payment pages.

While I was in Liberia, my friend Avani (who grew up in Zimbabwe) had to talk me down from a moment of self-doubt. In the process of restoring my baseline nihilism, she pointed out that in the end, what my angst amounts to for Africa is nothing. For me, this road trip represented countries number eighty-five to ninety-three. That might mean something significant for the pins on my cork globe

– but isn't particularly interesting by itself. In other words, I would come and go, and Africa and her people would remain Africa, as eternal and unaffected as ever.

"There have been times," she wrote from thousands of miles away in New York, "where I've made an honest effort to step up for those in Africa who aren't having their opinions heard, like I knew their opinions and professed myself their advocate. Maybe it's just because of the intense feeling Mama Africa gives every single person that visits Her."

"But here's the thing about Africa. Everyone has feelings about it, moreso than any other continent. Everyone thinks they have a say. Truth is probably none of us do. It is, undoubtably, the continent that needs the most attention and it deserves to be pulled up to everyone else's playing field."

DID THAT SENEGALESE MAN ON THE PLANE SMELL AWFUL?

Absolutely. But his dashiki was also very beautiful.

Ultimately, the problem is that we often don't say what we directly see, hear, and experience. We say what one says about the matter. And nowhere is that truer than of Africa, while at the same time, nowhere more than in Africa should a betrayal of authenticity be more unacceptable.

What I present to you are nine short stories from forty days in West Africa. The stories can be read consecutively, separately, or preferably not at all. At first, I had intended for the stories to be fictional, based on events that could have happened, but did not. After all, life in North America is usually predictable, so I could have no expectation that Africa would present me with not just one story, but *ten*. Because, when I set out, I had no real concept of what Africa was.

As time wore on, it became clear that my imagination would be meagre competition for the unpredictability of the journey. Most of my time was spent frantically transcribing contemporaneous conversations, nearly verbatim, and documenting sounds, smells, and sensations.

I spent an inordinate amount of time deciding whether any of my stories amounted to cultural appropriation. In the end, I decided they did not, since in most cases, neither Melody nor I have any idea what is really going on, nor do we presume to.

There are a mix of positive and negative stories, of stories that move and stories that stand still – and hints of my own happily nihilistic worldview, which my mother will need to graciously tolerate.

Are the stories true? Well, they're true enough. True enough for what, you might ask, and that's a fair question. As true as a cinematic adaptation of a novel, I suppose. But more importantly, *true enough* to represent one experience of Africa – honestly, and hopefully without being unfair to its people.

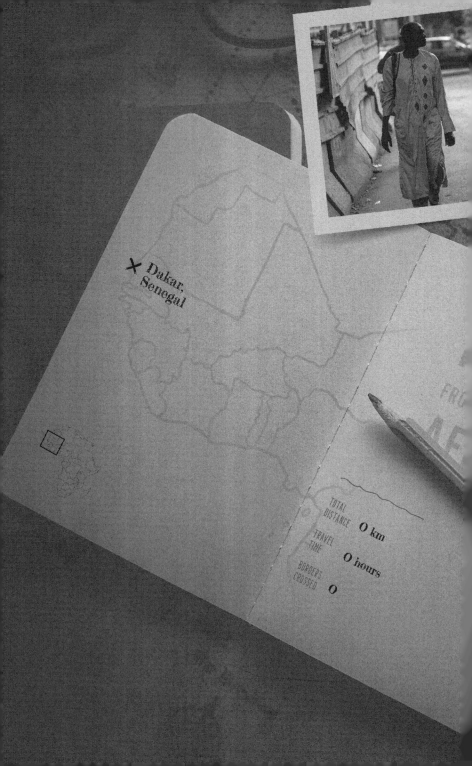

**✕ Dakar,
Senegal**

TOTAL
DISTANCE   **0 km**

TRAVEL
TIME   **0 hours**

BORDERS
CROSSED   **0**

M*balax* music, French bookstores, a surprisingly competent salsa night, and a fruitless search for *thiéboudienne* (the national Senegalese dish) — Senegal feels as though the Middle East suddenly met the Caribbean, simultaneously conservative, brash, and joyous. This short story is a composite of many sensory experiences, characters, and scenes encountered during our three days in Northern Senegal, told from the perspective and voice of a street hustler in Dakar. That means that while the individual elements of the story are true, the entirety of the story is not. However, in an abstract way, the story might also represent a sort of *condensed truth*, distilled for your approval. That said, in the end, this imagined tale isn't really about anything more than simply being present in the roiling chaos of Dakar.

LE ROI DU CARREFOUR

WE ARE ASSEMBLED ON THE MESSY STONE STEPS OF THIS downtown mosque, and around us, the unkempt market hums. This is one of the busiest intersections in Dakar, and a great unbroken crowd ebbs and flows past.

The men who encircle me on the steps are all what you might call hustlers. I will also call myself a hustler, but it is important for you to understand that I am an expert at my craft. If this were not so, I could not call myself the *roi du carrefour*. To foreigners who speak French poorly, this means that I am the *king of this intersection*.

Around my hustler friends, you will notice another circle of many other men, and those men mostly sell scuffed and dirty sneakers. Some of the shoes hang by their laces from an upright plank of wood, while others are carefully lined up along the curb. These men are sitting in plastic chairs wearing their colourful *dashikis* and waiting for customers. It is late in the afternoon now, so there are also devout men praying with foreheads face down on blankets. Ragged men and old women sitting beside the road in their wheelchairs, watching the world go by. Beggars too, but they are the few. It is not begging if you have something to offer, and almost everybody has something to offer.

Look closer and you will see women walking alone, navigating the crowd in their brightly coloured dresses and headdresses. Look down and there are women cooking meals in pots on the sidewalk. They are cooking here because is too hot to cook indoors, and besides, they would quickly choke on the thick clouds of smoke that come from their stoves.

A white Frenchman wearing a yellow *dashiki* and a thick moustache is passing us by. The yellow *dashiki* is very strange. It is like he wants to look African, even though he is not. To me, he looks foolish. This man looks young, but he has hollow, sunken eyes, and he is smoking a cigarette with a pale and bony hand that has too many veins. He walks beside an older white man who is wearing a black shirt. The black shirt fits like he is wearing a parachute, and it billows out at the bottom, as if he had once tried to tuck it in but then became distracted by something more important.

My friend next to me has his eye on these two foreign men. My friend wears a scarf on his head, his own traditional *dashiki* outfit, and his dark sunglasses. His earrings are made from somebody's old keys. I often ask him if he feels hot wearing all these clothes, but he says it is part of his look. His look gives him the attention he needs as an artist. I can understand this, because after all, my friend sells figurines made from garbage.

The white Frenchman has stopped to inspect my friend's merchandise. He leans forward, because the artwork is on the ground, wooden boards propped up against the curb. It seems he is looking at one that is the image of a woman, but not just any woman. Her body is made from an old calculator, her arms from bent pieces of rebar, and her head from bits of telephone. She is glued to a painted wooden board, just like the other pieces in his collection.

"They are slaves of technology," my friend explains.

"Very original," says the Frenchman. The parachute shirt man stands some distance behind him. He is not interested. Maybe he has been to Senegal before.

"Thank you," says my friend.

The Frenchman is wrong, however. The woman made from garbage is not original, and many Senegalese hustlers make things just like them and then sell them on the street. Why, there are at least ten more men selling the same thing on the next block. They are still garbage, but many tourists seem to enjoy taking this garbage home with them. For them, it is a happy memory of my country.

The Frenchman crouches down to inspect the calculator woman more carefully. He touches her calculator body and then looks at his own hand in disgust, because the garbage has left some dust on his fingertip. Then he takes his phone out of his pocket and taps the screen once. Twice. Three times.

My friend does not like this.

"You cannot just take photos," says my friend, and stands up quickly from his stoop. "You must either delete them or I will report you to the police. Show me."

I don't always understand these white people, but I do know that they like to take pictures. I don't always understand the things they take pictures of, because sometimes they are ugly things. But the pictures are very precious to them. I have even heard that when foreigners go home, they can sell these pictures to travel magazines for money. Money for them, that is. Still no money for us.

My friend looks over the Frenchman's shoulder as he cycles through his camera photos and deletes some of them. When he has finished, my friend nods, satisfied. The Frenchman seems to play with his hair nervously. Then he walks away without buying anything, and the parachute shirt man walks away with him, laughing.

"If they do not buy, then I do not let them take pictures," my friend says to me after the men have left.

ONE MUST ALWAYS BE PERSISTENT. IF A PERSON IS NOT PER-
sistent, then he does not sell and he becomes desperate.
And when a person becomes desperate, that person eventually ends up hungry.

This is man's work, of course. Men wander in and out of
the intersection carrying prayer blankets, table mats, fishing
rods, clothes hangers, smartphone cases, and car seat covers.
Few of us have enough money to buy a store, and so we sell
the things we can find, the things we can afford. But on the
other hand, I do not sell anything. I only fix things for people.

There is another white man walking down the street
now, and this one is holding the hand of a white woman.
My friend gets up again. He picks up one of his garbage
bracelets, and an earring that is made from an old key.

"Hello, my friend! What is your name?"

This white man smiles broadly and immediately meets
his gaze. He lets my friend approach him with his arm
outstretched in order to shake his hand.

"Lars," says the white man, still smiling warmly.

"Where are you from?" says my friend.

"Denmark," says the white man, and he accepts my
friend's handshake. As he does so, my friend skillfully bal-
ances a wooden beaded bracelet atop the white man's hand
as they connect. It is like magic. The white man looks surprised but has no choice but to accept it or throw it to the
ground. My friend is original. Inventive.

"*C'est un cadeau.*"

That is not true, of course, because a gift is something that you keep and never pay for. Giving gifts is very bad business. Lars from Denmark seems to know this and stops smiling. He is trying to give the bracelet back to my friend now, but my friend will not take it.

They will argue for awhile, and in the end my friend will never sell his bracelet. Sometimes my friend will even chase them down the street for many blocks until they become angry with him. I have seen all this before.

A TALL, LANKY FIGURE APPROACHES NOW. HE IS CLEAN, from head to toe. Wearing a solid black t-shirt and jeans. Not dusty. He is not quite a white man, but he is also not yet tanned. That means he could have only just arrived in Africa. He could be Brazilian, or Dominican, or Cuban. Perhaps Arab. In the end, it doesn't really matter.

I announce my presence while I walk towards him, approaching him directly on his right side. I draw myself up to my full height so that he knows that I deserve his attention.

"*Je suis le roi du carrefour.* What are you looking for?"

He hesitates, reluctant to make eye contact. Anybody who has been in Dakar longer than one day knows that you should not make eye contact with a hustler like me. I am not offended. If you answered every shout and call on the street, you would never get anywhere in this city. But I can tell this man's pace has slowed slightly.

"I need a battery," he says, although he still does not meet my eyes. "Do you sell battery chargers?"

"Of course I sell battery chargers," I say without hesitation.

He stops and looks behind me skeptically, as if he is expecting to see a battery store. He is skeptical because I am not holding any battery chargers, nor for that matter am I holding anything at all. I am just another man standing in the street, perhaps taller than most other men.

"Tell me what are you looking for?" I repeat, and only now does he look me in the face.

Even so, it is almost like he is looking through me. He is so suspicious. But they are almost always suspicious, and in the end, he unslings his backpack and reaches into a side pocket to produce a small object that fits inside his palm.

"Do you sell a battery charger for this?"

"Of course," I say to him. "I will take a picture of this."

I take my phone out of my pocket. Then, I take a picture of his battery, which is a peculiar rectangular black thing. It looks like it belongs inside one of those enormous cameras that tourists carry.

"*Attends-ici.*" I pause and inspect him. He is glancing around the market and I can tell he won't wait here long, which means I don't have much time. I run into the crowd, into the dust of central Dakar. Past the cars whose wind-shields are also covered in dust. Past the tires. Past the piles of rubble and dirt. On a side street, there are grubby children playing air hockey. I run past them too.

I know where there is a wholesale shop that will sell his battery charger. It is by far the best electronics store in town.

Past the yellow and black taxis. Past the vendors with wheeled carts who sell insecticide and rat poison. And especially past one spacious and elegant store called *NovaTek*, because only a tourist or a rich man would ever shop there. At *NovaTek*, there is lots of room to walk around inside, but in my opinion, not enough *stuff*. I should know this because I used to work there not long ago, and I would have to sneak away to the wholesale shop to sell items to my customers. The boss did not like this.

Yes, this wholesale shop. From a distance, it looks like a garage, if that garage were only the size of a closet. Perhaps it would be deep enough to park a motorcycle inside, if the space were not already a jumble of boxes and plastic or metal parts. Every corner is filled with electronic odds and ends, and between the crevices, the owner has managed to wedge even tinier objects inside. There is no sign or awning above this shop, but instead there is a fat man with a white beard next to the curb. Legs crossed, he is resting on a pink plastic chair that looks like it is ready to break.

I show him the picture of the rectangular battery and he pinches the screen to look closer at its markings.

"Yes, I have."

He rocks himself out of his plastic chair and ambles to the garage. Then he wedges his potbelly into the only remaining space and rummages behind him. It takes him no longer than twenty seconds to emerge triumphant with a small, unmarked box. He opens it, briefly inspects the plastic object inside, and hands it to me.

"This is the one."

He has never once disappointed me.

WHEN I RUN BACK TO THE STEPS OF THE MOSQUE, THE TALL not-quite white man is still there, standing patiently. I exhale.

I show him the unmarked box, then extract the rectangular battery charger, and a power cable.

"How did you do that?" he says. His eyebrows go up, and he is smiling. Now he is looking me directly in my eyes. He is looking at me like I am a magician, as if I just made a white dove appear in my hand from thin air.

"That is my job. I know the market in and out."

"*C'est incroyable.*"

"*Doucement,*" I say as I gingerly thread the prongs of the plug into the wall outlet. He fits the rectangular battery into the hollow of the charger and it immediately lights up. So does this tourist's face. I have him now.

"*C'est combien, ça?*"

He wants to know how much it is, but it is clear now that I have the thing he needs. That means the price is however much I say it is. As long as I don't get greedy.

"Forty dollars." I look away from him. I have learned to control my body language.

The tourist is still smiling at me. He reaches into his pocket and pulls out an ugly fabric wallet. Then he begins to babble at me in broken French.

"I didn't think I would ever be able to find this charger here. I don't see anybody carrying this kind of camera. I just don't know how you found this."

It is perhaps too late to raise the price even more, so I only smile back at him and take his money. It has been a good day.

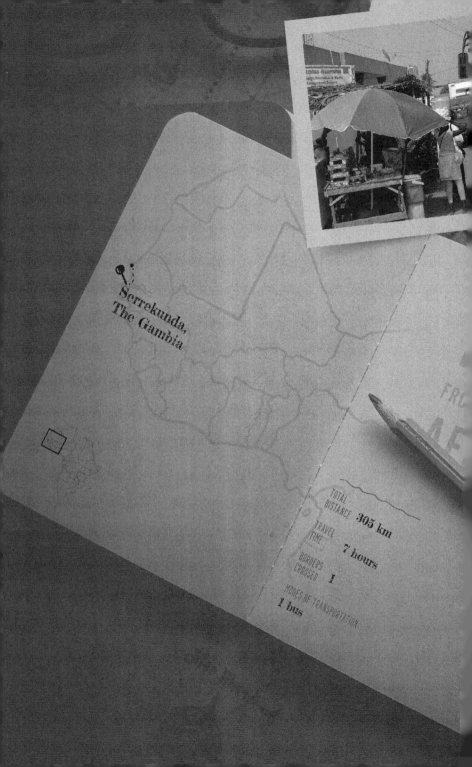

Serrekunda,
The Gambia

TOTAL
DISTANCE **305 km**

TRAVEL
TIME **7 hours**

BORDERS
CROSSED **1**

MODES OF TRANSPORTATION
1 bus

This short story approaches being entirely truthful and describes, in intentionally excessive detail, an ill-fated bus journey across the land border between Dakar and Serrekunda. Once again, the setting is the essence of the story, and my hopes are that by the end, you too will be eager to get off this hot bus. The story is ultimately about time wasted – both ours and possibly yours – but also about the acceptance that a journey (especially in Africa) might be more important than its destination.

MAYBE
48 DEGREES

THEY SAY THAT IF YOU LEAVE DAKAR EARLY IN THE MOR-
ning, you'll make it to Serrekunda by noon. With some
luck, you'll be on the beach by mid-afternoon. And if it's a
day trip you've planned, you could even be back in Dakar
by evening.

Serrekunda is the largest city on the implausibly tiny
sliver of land known as The Gambia, which is nestled between Northern and Southern Senegal. For now, our coach
bus has parked itself at the border post in a town called
Barra. It's already two o'clock in the afternoon.

In Spanish, the literal translation of the name Barra
would be *mud*. In West Africa, I can't be sure what the
word means, but I'm certain that if it rained, it would definitely be muddy. In the dry season of the here and now,
however, Barra remains mainly dirt and dust.

There is no chaos quite like the chaos of a land border. Unlike an airport, a land border is never the public face of a nation, never the first impression that diplomats and presidents experience when they visit your country. It's the airport that serves that purpose – that ideal, impeccably groomed version of yourself that you present on a first date or a job interview. In contrast, a land border is what your close friends see when they show up to your house unannounced, and promptly decide to inspect the bathroom.

All this would be true anywhere in the world, but it is especially true of West Africa. At this particular border post, dozens of unaccompanied children are milling about, greeting and chasing after emerging passengers, hands outstretched as they solicit money. A startled goat trots away from us as we follow our group through the congestion and toward the customs building.

I identify several landmarks, who silently lead the way. Near the front, Man with Yankees Cap is followed by Woman Wearing Yellow Blouse. In the middle of the pack, there is Skinny Man with Blue Shirt. There is a hen who joins us in line as we wait patiently. But at least there is a semblance of order amid the chaos.

It isn't long before a border agent welcomes us into his office and beckons us to sit down. He isn't dressed in any particularly official uniform. He's just a guy behind a rough wooden desk. He banters with us as if we are friends of friends.

"Canada is very nice country," he says. "I have seen the pictures. First time to come to The Gambia?"

Melody and I nod and smile blandly as we push our passports across the desk. We have previously agreed that bland, inoffensive, and friendly are all desirable traits for any tourist crossing a West African land border.

"You will enjoy it. My name is Moses."

"It's nice to meet you, Moses," says Melody.

"People wondering why The Gambia is so peaceful," says Moses. "We have *dan kuto*. It means *friendly joking relationship*. We will talk bad about each other's mother, and then come to an agreement. If someone is Fula tribe, I can tell him he is ugly. I can eat all his food."

We laugh. Moses flips through our documents. Then he looks up again, beaming.

"But there are protests in The Gambia. The president has to go. His three-year term is up. You will find it very difficult finding a car from Banjul to Serrekunda."

"Oh," I say. That doesn't sound peaceful at all. Perhaps this is part of his *dan kuto*. "Well that's not good, is it?"

"Thank you for telling us, Moses," says Melody.

He stamps our passports. We have officially entered The Gambia.

WE BOARD THE COACH BUS AGAIN, BUT IT DOESN'T TAKE US far. This time, the driver stops at a ferry terminal, where a boat will carry our bus across the river and into the capital city of Banjul. Melody, who is reliably less sanguine than myself about this type of thing, has already researched this.

"Okay, so the British Foreign Office doesn't love this ferry," Melody announces, scrolling down the pane of her phone.

"Huh. Why not?"

"It says it has a poor safety record. It says: 'the boats are old, overcrowded, and sometimes break down mid-cross-ing'."

"Well, that's not good either, is it?"

"'Local boatmen operate pirogues as an alternative to the ferry and to attract tourist traffic. They are often over-loaded and sometimes sink during the crossing. It's unlike-ly they will have life jackets.'"

"Uh huh. What's a pirogue?"

"I think it's like a little sketchy canoe."

That's enough of that, I decide. If this boat is good enough for the Gambians, then it is good enough for us – ignoring those numerous times that it was demonstrably not good enough even for the Gambians. I can't help but acknowledge that '*Ferry disaster kills 63, two Canadians in The Gambia*' might only warrant a page eight headline in the West, squeezed somewhere between plans for a new downtown skateboard park and the daily crossword. That seems vaguely disappointing, but then again, post-mortem headlines only matter to those alive to read them. Humans are naturally drawn to stage an epic drama of the significance of their own lives. I suppose it's a harmless conceit.

"When you Google 'Banjul Barra ferry', the search box just autocompletes to 'Banjul Barra ferry accident'."

Okay, stop please.

A sliver of the ferry dock is just visible beyond the crowds of gathered vendors and food stalls. Aboard our coach bus, the Muslim women around us are standing up in their seats and shouting in their Wolof language. One wears a colourful and extravagant headdress and carries a large plastic washbasin with a Guess purse inside. Another wears glasses, several gold bracelets, and is wrapped in a silk scarf. She is praying with a wooden rosary, or at least she was doing so before the shouting began. Now that rosary is slung loosely around her wrist, and it whips back and forth as she gesticulates to the others.

"What do you think they're yelling about?" asks Melody.

I shrug. Probably nothing important.

There is a prominent digital thermometer at the front of the bus, just above the windshield, above the driver's head. It had escaped my attention before, but without the breeze and the changing African scenery outside our window, there are fewer distractions to contend with now. The thermometer ticks upward from forty-five to forty-six degrees.

That couldn't be right. It's hot, but not *that* hot.

It shouldn't be long before the ferry leaves. And so, we wait.

MBALAX IS PLAYING OVER THE SPEAKERS IN THE BUS, AND the man beside us has struck up a conversation. The first thing he explains is how to pronounce the word *mbalax*. It sounds like *balakh* – the first consonant receding into an imperceptible hum, like the low drone of bagpipes, and the ending of the word harsh and guttural. The music itself is frantic and busy. It's hard to conceive of a form of music less suited to waiting patiently in a hot, stationary bus.

"I am here from Guinea for hustling," he explains to us. "I cannot go back. It is a complicated story. It is three years I no see my family. Now I play *kora* every night at a hotel."

He wears a Yankees cap, and carries a peculiar string instrument that looks like a rounder version of a guitar, if that guitar had somehow been impregnated.

We ask him what we are waiting for, because it's now been an hour at this ferry crossing, and the stifling bus still shows no signs of life. What's more, it is only half full now.

Many of the passengers have abandoned the sweaty vehicle and are milling about outside.

"There are demonstrations on the other side, so we don't know what time the boat will come."

"One way or another, this bus will end up in Serrekunda," I suggest to him. "It's only a matter of time, right?"

Yankees cap agrees.

The thermometer ticks upward to forty-seven degrees.

Forty-eight degrees.

It's four o'clock now, five hours since we left our hotel in Dakar. It's hot, an enveloping, embracing heat that creates a lethargy that extends from head to toe. I suppose ordinary vacationers pay good money to escape their air-conditioned cubicles in the sky to sit motionless in a place where the weather is consistently forty-eight degrees and muggy.

If I close my eyes here, I can imagine we are already on the beach.

A FLATBED TRUCK LOADED WITH MILITARY MEN WEARING green and yellow camouflage passes in front of our bus. Some of the men are standing, others are crouched, and a few are sitting, their legs dangling over the sides. Most appear bored, looking backwards with indifference at the growing congestion of dozens of waiting vehicles. The arrival of the military has never been a particularly good omen, and I make my way to the front of the bus to ask the driver when he thinks our boat will arrive. He is standing outside the doorway with the skinny man in the blue shirt.

"It still not coming," he says. "Maybe one hour."

"Maybe," I say, unconvinced. "Why are they protesting anyway?"

"They are protesting the president. The constitution says five years. But the protesters, they don't like him, they want him to step down after three years."

"So you think he should stay? Did you vote for the president?"

"I have never voted," says the driver. "I think politics is dirty. I will not waste my time and energy. Most people, they don't want anything to do with the protest. But some people, they useless. They jobless. Their friend is going to the protest, so they go along."

Skinny man in blue shirt nods sagely.

It all sounds very complicated, and I'm in no position to untangle this complex web of Gambian politics. Likewise, I imagine that all this man would like to do is drive his bus back and forth across the river and be paid for his efforts, which seems perfectly reasonable. Whoever ends up in power in Banjul, they will still need a bus to be driven across the river. But if the driver is annoyed by the delay, he is either too world-weary to let it show, similarly subdued by the inevitable heat, or too captivated by his conversation with the skinny man in the blue shirt.

"I'm going outside," I suddenly announce to Melody. I'm hot and hungry, and we have now been squeezed into this cramped seat for six hours.

When I do so, I bring my daypack with me. It would be foolish not to, given the realities of *backpack separation syndrome*, a well-documented psychological affliction in the frequent traveler. Backpack separation syndrome refers to the entirely justified belief that one is never more than a single false move from being forever separated from our passport, money, and phone, and to a lesser extent, our clothes and clean underwear. When I return from this minor expedition, the bus may well have disappeared without a trace, leaving me with only my identity and enough cash to get home.

Outside the bus, throngs of merchants are selling fruits, fish, and vegetables in wicker baskets. Women pass by carrying or balancing boxes, bags, and buckets. A man behind hisses as he squeezes past, pushing a wheelbarrow filled with shoes. A guard wearing a tattered uniform waves me through a rusted metal gate, and I follow a flight of stairs up and into the second-floor restaurant that overlooks the ferry dock.

The waitress is sprawled across the counter when I enter, her head partially buried in the crook of her elbow. A housefly rests comfortably on her forehead. She raises her head only slightly when I advance, enough to notice that she has only one sighted eye. The other is grey and cloudy.

Her presence intimidates me. Maybe I'm intruding.

Garbage is strewn across the floor of the restaurant. I approach the counter and thumb through the dusty laminated menu. There's no time to wait for a full meal. By now, I half-expect that our bus has already crossed the river and arrived in Banjul.

"Two vegetable pies, please."

"The vegetables will take time."

"Meat is fine. And two bottles of water." Africa is no place for a vegetarian. I'm no vegetarian but even so, fending off scurvy remains a worthy goal. We have quickly caught on that green vegetables will rarely appear in West Africa without specific efforts. You're more likely to find some variation of rice, meat, and plantain, nestled under a blanket of sauce.

The waitress slowly rises to her feet, as if her body is being crushed by the heat. She scuffs her feet against the floor as she shuffles towards the kitchen. Then she returns, sits, and props her head upon her folded arms atop the counter. There is an uncomfortable silence.

"What is going on outside?" I ask hesitantly.

Her face remains expressionless and her affect flat, as if she is bored and this attempt at conversation is barely worthy of her effort. She looks back again towards the kitchen, as if awaiting rescue. But when she responds, it is in a loud whisper.

"The president. I have to reduce my voice because there are some people who don't like him."

"I see."

"The president made verbal agreement to leave after three years, but the constitution says five years. So now he want to stay. But he had backing from the biggest party, so now they want to throw him out."

"But you think it would be fine if he stayed in office."

She nods, but her expression does not change. I don't press her any further, although it doesn't seem very *dan kuto* to hide one's feelings about who should or should not be president.

SOMEHOW, THE BUS IS STILL THERE, EXACTLY WHERE I LEFT it. It is as though time has stopped, as if the sands of an hourglass were exchanged for warm molasses. Of course, time has done no such thing. We've been at the ferry crossing for three hours when I return to our seats carrying two warm paper bags.

"We live here now," Melody says cheerfully. I present her with two meat pies. They are delicious.

"When you were gone," she continues, "a girl came up to the window, and she wanted to know if I wanted fish.

I looked at it, and the fish were in a bucket on her head. I probably would have bought it if it weren't a bucket of warm fish on her head."

I agree with her that declining to eat the warm fish was a good call. We have seven countries left, and it's both too early for dysentery and also never the right time. Besides, these meat pies taste better than they have any right to, considering their source. I should have brought one for the *kora* man beside us, but he is no longer in his seat.

Once again, the Muslim ladies are becoming impatient. The one behind me is shouting and slamming her fist on the back of my seat. I turn behind me and glance at her.

"Sorry," says the woman in English, and the others laugh.

"Why is she mad?"

"She's always mad," says Melody. "She doesn't mean it. She just is."

THE ENGINE STARTS, AND SCATTERED CHEERS ERUPT ACROSS the bus. The *kora* man rushes in through the back door, swings up the rails and into his seat. There is a jerk, and then we begin to inch forward past the vendors and finally, onto the waiting ferry.

Forty-four degrees. Forty-two. Thirty-seven. By now the heat aboard the bus has receded to a state of comfortable warmth, like a sunny day. It's six o'clock now, and we've been aboard this bus for seven hours. The ferry crossing is anticlimactic, passing imperceptibly until we suddenly find ourselves coasting down the smooth tarmac of highway carved between the tiny capital city of Banjul and the metropolis of Serrekunda. On either side of the highway, the forest is relentlessly dense, until it remits all at once and gives way to progressively larger structures. Then, at a bus stop that could be anywhere or nowhere, we emerge from the bus in the twilight, cradling our oversized backpacks.

The taxi rank that greets us is a cluster of haphazardly parked cars, their drivers waiting for the tired passengers to disembark. We select a car at random and agree to pay whatever price the driver suggests.

"Your English is very good!" Melody says to the driver once we are settled in the back seat. "You must meet lots of British people."

"Yes, English and French," our amiable driver agrees. "Most people who come to The Gambia, they are British. They come to sit on the beach. But most people here do not speak good English because they do not go to school. If they work in a hotel, or in a taxi, they speak English. But other people, they only speak the tribal language."

He gives us the news on the way to our hotel. Three protesters were killed today in Banjul. Hundreds more were gassed by the police. He seems neither bothered, excited, frightened, nor surprised.

"Will there be protests again tomorrow?" I ask him.

"No," says the taxi driver. "The protesters are very tired. *C'est fini*. It will be safe for you to explore Serrekunda. But tell me, why would you come all the way here from Canada to The Gambia?"

We certainly didn't come for the beach. Maybe we came for exactly the opposite. We came to sit inside a hot bus listening to *mbalax* for hours with a *kora* player and several women shouting furiously in Wolof, and to eat meat pies. In the right frame of mind, today could be described as a quintessential African experience.

"I guess you could call it a cultural trip," Melody finally responds.

"So what did we learn today?" I ask Melody as we pull up to the hotel.

"I don't know if we learned anything, except that *dan kuto* is mostly theoretical. Or at least, it doesn't mean anything very specific."

"True," I say. "I mean, it was more interesting than sitting on the beach, that's for sure."

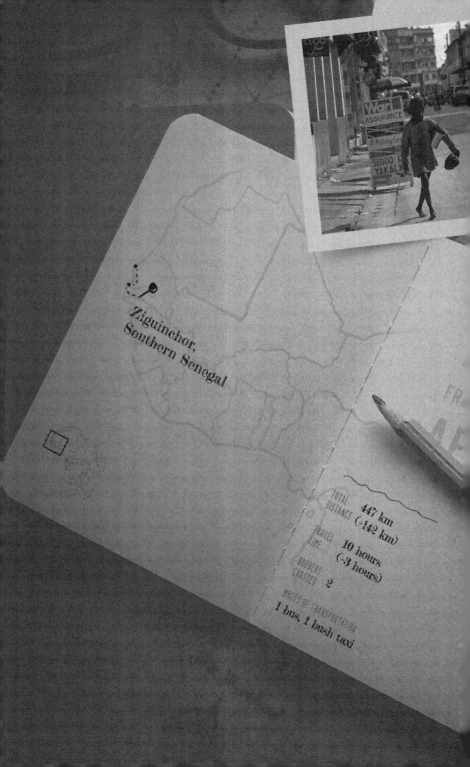

Ziguinchor,
Southern Senegal

TOTAL
DISTANCE   **447 km**
           (+142 km)

TRAVEL
TIME   **10 hours**
           (-3 hours)

BORDERS
CROSSED   **2**

MODES OF TRANSPORTATION
1 bus, 1 bush taxi

U nlike Dakar and Serrekunda, far fewer travelers make it to Southern Senegal (and specifically, into the dusty town of Ziguinchor). This short story emerged from a series of conversations in Ziguinchor about the complex ethics of giving money to the omnipresent street children roaming the city centre. The story is mostly true – but somewhat heavy and philosophical, and therefore, there is a good chance my mother will not like it.

SANCTUARY

THE TRANSIT PARK IN ZIGUINCHOR IS A SEA OF UNMANAGED humanity. When we emerge from our cramped seats and battered bush taxi, we are confronted by beggars clattering sticks inside calabash half shells, and those half shells are half filled with change and petty cash. Not far beyond, a loudspeaker mounted to the roof of a van is bellowing something muffled and incomprehensible in what seems to be Arabic.

We decide to walk from the station to our hotel, not only because doing so will build character, but also because exploring on foot is the best way to experience a place. Something about the sensation of pavement under moving feet creates that instinctive internal map more efficiently than a ride in the back of a taxi ever could. Neurons fire. Synapses form. However, an afternoon walk anywhere in

West Africa means there is no refuge from the oppressive heat, nor the blinding midday sun.

Ziguinchor itself is far from beautiful, but the locals continue about their routines, oblivious to their homely surroundings. Physical beauty and symmetry might be overrated values when the essence of your world consists of your business, your social circle, and your family. Perhaps beauty only matters to a tourist, and tourism doesn't seem to be high on the agenda here. But there is always something unique everywhere, if you care to look closely enough.

In Ziguinchor, that thing is tires.

Everywhere you look in Ziguinchor, you're likely to find a tire. When we first notice this, it's odd, but not astonishing. The coarse, pockmarked roads here aren't kind, and they don't bode well for the lifespan of a tire. But when that punctured, torn, or otherwise ruined flat is unceremoniously uncoupled from its vehicle, that milestone is only the beginning of its life here, not the end. Those broken tires serve as fences, chairs, and children's toys. They're weighty enough to hold signs down. Stacked one atop another, they can even be used as buckets or garbage cans. Ziguinchor might have more stray tires per capita than any other place in the world.

Come visit Ziguinchor, the town of ten thousand tires. But beautiful, no. Far from it.

An old man wearing traditional dress is locking the gate of what is presumably his home. He is shuffling slowly because in this crushing heat, there is never any hurry. His face is friendly, so we smile at him as our paths cross on the sidewalk. He turns and greets us too with a smile and a wave. Then he points to his feet.

"*Cuir*," he says. I think he also wants to sell us some leather.

"He's always hustling," Melody says to me. It's true. In Senegal, everybody is.

We've reached the town centre, represented by an un-assuming roundabout populated occasionally by circling automobiles and more frequently by pedestrians. Only a half block away, we encounter the Kassa restaurant, which our guidebook suggests as the main tourist sanctuary in Ziguinchor. Sure enough, the view through the doorway reveals a Western-style venue studded with varnished wooden tables and chairs surrounding a pleasant court-yard. It's not particularly beautiful, nor unique, but it does look comfortable.

As we peer inside from a modest distance, a mob of children move to crowd and block the doorway, their faded soccer jerseys stained brown with dust. They look about ten years old – maybe more, maybe less. The focus of their attention, a white Frenchman, exits the restaurant and they instinctively extend their hands, but don't pursue him. Their begging seems to be a learned behaviour, a conditioned Pavlovian response.

A waitress emerges and swats the children away like flies. They briefly disperse into the parking lot, and then reassemble long enough to approach the two of us with their hands out.

"Mister, give me money," says one, in English.

"No," says Melody, simply.

I shake my head as well, because I don't understand why a child would need to beg for money. It's distressing, but I remind myself that there is no urgency to this matter. I wasn't around yesterday when they were begging for money, although I will still be around tomorrow.

There is something about begging children that is viscerally distressing. Their innocence is presumed, so compassion is automatic. And because the existence of these begging children weighs on my conscience, I tell a friend at home about the mob of street children at the Kassa. She thinks that if she had been there, maybe she would have given them money.

"I know you can't solve the big problem," she says to me, "but you can give them some peace of mind for a few weeks, however long that extra money can last. You can't understand everything in life, or fix everything, and money is the least of it, but it always helps if only in the immediate future. Some things are just the way they are.

While you're trying to understand, they're living it in reality day by day."

That's not what Melody says. She feels no such obligation. If we give them money, they will just keep begging. They will learn that Westerners have money, and that they will part with it for nothing more than a smile and a tap on the shoulder. They will learn that their wretchedness wields a sort of power over adults. For children, everything is a lesson, nothing is without meaning – and this lesson is not one that nurtures independent, well-adjusted future citizens of the world.

Of course, we would never tolerate any of this wretchedness at home. But now that I think about it, I've also never encountered a begging child at home.

THE NEXT DAY, WE RETURN TO THE KASSA, AND THE SAME Frenchman is having beer and cigarettes at eight o'clock in the morning. I suppose beer and cigarettes are a necessity as an expat here, morning be damned. After all, the creature comforts of Ziguinchor are few and far between. I take stock of this gaunt man, with his grey hair, dark rimmed glasses, wrinkled jeans, and too-large pullover. A dull brown satchel rests on the floor next to his chair.

There is a certain haggard look that expatriates take on, like a sagging, condemned house on the edge of town. I wonder how long it takes for them to perfect this drooping appearance, and what conspiracy of circumstances would lead such a droopy European man to be dispatched to what is unequivocally the wrong side of Senegal.

"Who are those children outside the restaurant?" I ask him, worried I could be interrupting his morning sadness. "I mean, where are their parents?"

"*Les enfants de la rue?*" he says dismissively, extinguishing his cigarette in the ashtray. "They are street children, just like in any other place. They live on the street, they don't go to school, they just ask for money."

"It's a learned behaviour," repeats Melody, and the droopy man nods. "If you give them money, it only makes the problem worse."

TO CROSS THE SOUTHERN BORDER OF SENEGAL INTO GUINea Bissau tomorrow, Melody and I will need visas, and those visas in turn require a walk across town to the Bissau Guinean embassy.

Dozens of goats scurry away from us down the dirt road ahead. Alongside us, a boy chops wood with an axe in a yard bounded by a corrugated aluminum fence. On the opposite side of this fence, another man is either fixing his motorcycle or dismantling it. The bike looks less like a vehicle than a heap of metal fragments. Neither man pays the slightest attention to the four street children who are approaching, running. The children are yelling and laughing to each other.

When they reach us, one child stops, and the others rush past in a windmill of limbs. The one who stops raises two fingers to his mouth and speaks in hushed tones. The sudden shift in his demeanor is remarkable.

"*Pour manger*," he says. He's hungry. "*Monsieur Leblanc? S'il vous plaît?*"

"No," says Melody, simply.

"*Desolé*," I respond, and it's true. I am sorry – but for what exactly? And now that I stop to consider it, the street children are all boys. Where are the girls?

But I don't ask that.

"*Pourquoi tu n'es pas en école?*" I ask instead, since it is a weekday morning. Why aren't you in school?

The boy doesn't answer. He waits several seconds more, and then loses interest and pursues his friends down the road. Perhaps my tone was too accusatory. Perhaps he didn't like my French accent. Perhaps he just had no good answer.

"I don't think he would understand why someone would ask that," says Melody.

"I'm not sure about that. Give him some credit. I think he knows exactly what I'm asking."

We stroll further down the dirt road, and the sound of laughing children gradually diminishes. It occurs to me what awful, selfish people we are. We are making a virtue of the callousness of arriving in such a place and expecting to carry on as indifferent observers of the world that surrounds us, the world which unifies us all. That world is emotionally tiring.

In the pocket of my hiking pants, I am carrying enough money to line the frayed pockets of every child who extends his hand. But first, I would need to find a way to break my currency into smaller bills. Difficult, but not impossible. Soon, word of my goodwill would spread. The friends of these street children would chase after me like their pied piper for a share of the prize. I would give them money too, naturally, and their grateful smiles would be infectious. They would use the money to buy food, pencils and pens, and soccer balls. Tomorrow, Melody and I would leave Ziguinchor for Bissau, but the children would always remember the day that a generous white man arrived and gave them more hope than they had ever dreamed of.

We could be heroes.

"Should we wrap up some rice and give it to them next time?" asks Melody, rousing me from my daze.

I don't quite know the answer to that. For that matter, I don't know if they would appreciate rice as much as money.

SANCTUARY IS AN APT DESCRIPTION FOR THE PLACES THAT Westerners frequent in West Africa. Westerners don't want to experience all of the magnificence of Africa, because we cannot possibly handle it – we can only handle Africa in short bursts. The differences between here and home are just too jarring. When that shock overwhelms us, we must retreat to our barracks, to our plush hotels fitted with metal detectors and security guards. The abrupt shift in tone is one from chaos to tranquility. Inside a sanctuary, there is a calming sense that time itself has suddenly stopped.

Rarely does any compromise exist between the two. There is international standard, and there is *African* standard. Volunteers and humanitarians and diplomats will not willingly lodge in African standard hotels, and they don't foot the bill for their accommodation anyway. They will only discuss how to fix the pressing problems outside from behind the secure walls of their sanctuaries.

This hotel in Ziguinchor is one such sanctuary, insulated from any of the tiring unpleasantness beyond its walls. It's not our hotel, because its price is the sort that one would only ever expense to *somebody else*, never willingly pay out of pocket. On the lovingly manicured lawn stands a beautiful, useless stylized copper statue of an elegant woman, and several metres away, an equally useless copper wheelbarrow. An appropriately elegant African woman, this one flesh and blood, is dressed in yellow and smiles as she walks through the gardens beside a white French businessman. On the wooden pier, umbrellas sprout from planters that cast shadows over the symmetric tables of

the restaurant. The service is disinterested, and the pout-
ing waitresses mope their way from table to table. We sit,
alternately sipping espresso and wine in the shade, while
waves lap at the edges of the boardwalk.

Three immaculately dressed Africans sit around the
table behind us, and they speak in perfectly refined French.
It is the delicate French of an educated class more European than African, but I would never suggest that out loud.
The stillness of the air allows me to hear and understand
their conversation in its entirety. It seems they will be pan-
elists tomorrow evening at the Alliance Française in central
Ziguinchor. There, they will be the featured speakers at an
academic forum discussing existentialism.

Even now, they are animated as they discuss the important things – what it means to be alive in this world,
what our individual roles might be in this great enterprise
of our species. Their voices rise and fall as they wrestle with
the nature of consciousness, emotion, and the importance
of memories. The question of where we are going as a human race and who are we becoming. Things weighty and
profound. It will be an important debate once they manage
to squeeze past the begging children at the gates.

BACK AT OUR OWN HOTEL, WE NEED TO ASK AGAIN, BECAUSE
we didn't understand the first time.

In Egypt, a taxi driver once told me about the import-

ance of asking for anything *at least three times*, and preferably to at least three different people – since on at least one
of those occasions, a person will tell you something demonstrably false, simply to be seen as polite and helpful. In
Africa, it's equally important to ask everything three times.
Once, to decipher the language. Twice, to understand the
nuances. Three times, to then appreciate that you will still
never understand the nuances.

Nevertheless, the receptionist seems vaguely irritated
by our curiosity about the roving gangs of street children.

"So, it's a school then?" I try to clarify.

"No," she says in French. "In the morning, the children look for money. At six o'clock in the evening, they go
back to the house. It's not school. It's a house."

"Almost like a night school?"

"No," she repeats. "It's not a school the way you think.
They have rooms for the children."

"Do they have to pay?"

"No. No."

But the concept of some sort of boarding school in
which children beg for money is just the clue Melody
needs to research it later that evening. From what she
gleans, Islamic families whose resources are stretched send
their children into town to learn the Qur'an. In the morning, they beg. At night, they study their holy book. Most
have parents. Some don't. It is a common enough practice

both here and in northern Nigeria, where *almajaris* run by *mallams* (teachers) count almost seven million pupils.

"So there's no problem here, and this is all just a cultural thing that we've never heard of?" I clarify, laying on my back and staring up at the ceiling of our hotel room. "Islamic boot camp?"

"I guess?" says Melody. "I just wonder how we didn't notice any of this in Dakar. But to be fair, I guess we weren't really looking for it."

THE KASSA ALSO MAKES A GOOD PLACE FOR AN EVENING COFfee, in that it is perhaps the only place in town for an evening coffee. When we arrive at half past nine at night, the street children are still prowling outside the entrance. They helpfully open the door of our taxi, and then become a kaleidoscope of many hands probing our shoulders, legs, and backs. A wall of grasping and pleading hands reaching towards us.

They shouldn't still be here, because it's well past six o'clock. That's what we were just told only hours ago – and although we were told in French, it's frustrating to believe I could have mangled the translation so badly. They should be *home* at the boarding school, that school which obviously isn't so much of a school as we might think.

Safely inside the sanctuary, the lights are unusually dim and there is no music. We settle at the bar, apparently the only customers in this cavernous and empty room. It gives the restaurant the distinct atmosphere of a place on the verge of closing, possibly forever. As the waiter approaches, I feel some guilt over interrogating him about the most visible sign of poverty and decay in the social fabric of Senegal, so I wait until he has delivered our espressos.

"Shouldn't they be home now?" I ask, and nod towards the door.

"Normally, yes," says the waiter. "But if they don't return with at least five hundred francs, they get beaten." He makes a whipping motion with his hand.

"That's terrible."

"Yes, it's terrible."

Five hundred Senegalese francs is little more than a dollar. It puts the matter in a somewhat different perspective. For the cost of a cup of coffee, you can feed a hungry child. For the cost of a cup of coffee, we can stop another one from being beaten. It's a comfortably simple construction, convenient as instant pancake mix, in which the problems of the world are easily within our grasp. Just add money.

"Does the restaurant ever give food to the street children?" Melody asks. "Maybe some rice, wrapped up?"

"Yes, of course. Every day in the afternoon there is a box that we give them."

Rice will extinguish the pangs of hunger, but I wonder if rice will stop the beatings as effectively as money. I'm not convinced it will.

WE LEAVE ZIGUINCHOR THE FOLLOWING MORNING.

As we navigate the sidewalk to return to the transit park, two more street children cross our path. One wears comically oversized shoes that flap against the ground with every step, while the other wears no shoes at all. At the moment of contact, they briefly turn towards us to hold their hands out, and once rebuffed, they continue on their way. I realize nothing has changed since our first day here.

"Do you want to give them money now?" I ask Melody. "I mean, now that we know that they're being exploited by these religious schools?"

"No."

"Why not?"

"Because if the school depends on the money, and we don't give it to them, then eventually, maybe this model where children have to beg on the street will fall apart."

Of course, we both know that nothing will fall apart based on our presence for two days in Ziguinchor. But her point still stands.

"Imagine you came across a World Vision commercial," I respond, "and that commercial told you that for only a dollar a day, you could put a roof over a child's head, but that the child would be beaten regularly, and they would roam the streets all day wearing rags and no shoes. And you would have no transparency over where that dollar actually went. Would you give to that charity?"

"No." She pauses to consider the matter further. Maybe this is all an elaborate mental construction to ease our own Western guilt. "But I still feel bad about it."

**Bissau,
Guinea Bissau**

TOTAL
DISTANCE **593 km
(+146 km)**

TRAVEL
TIME **13 hours
(+3 hours)**

BORDERS
CROSSED **3**

MODES OF TRANSPORTATION
**1 bus, 3 bush taxis,
1 motorcycle, 1 canoe**

CONSULADO GERAL
DA GUINÉ - BISSAU
EM ZIGUINCHOR E KOLDA
VISTO Nº 185 20 20
(Visa *Éverée)*
Nome completo CHRISTOPHER J. DANTON
(Nom complet)
Sexo H Nacionalidade CANADIANA
(Sexe) (Nationalité)
Nº de passaporte AH860125
(Nº du passeport)
Tipo de visto PORVIAL
(Type de visa)
Motivo de viagem TURISMO
(Motif de voyage)
Duração 30 dias com DIAS
(Durée)
Validade 30 (jours) (avec) Entrada (s)
(Validité) 30 / 02 / 2020 carée (s)
Emitido em 30, 01, 2020
(Délivré le)

22

There's a commonly held misconception that Africa is as a single homogenous entity – that even if some differences exist between Kenya and Senegal, then at least the countries *within* West Africa must be relatively similar. But that's neither true in language nor culture. For example, Senegal runs like a well-oiled machine. Guinea Bissau does not. And if you're looking for the guarantee of harrowing adventure, the best way to find it is to cross a remote land border between Guinea Bissau and Guinea by motorcycle. Just be sure to bring money. This is the entirely true story of the most emotionally taxing day in all my years of travelling, which will be equally taxing for my mother when she reads about it.

CADEAU

"HA! *E LONGE!*" SAYS THE DRIVER WHEN I ASK HOW LONG IT
will take to reach Conakry. "It is three hours just to reach
Quebo."

Conakry is the capital of Guinea but getting there will
involve a border crossing in a place that didn't exist to us
scant minutes ago. After Quebo comes Boké. These names
exist now only as points on a map, not as living, breathing
places. But the driver of this aging Mercedes has heard of
both these places, and he thinks the *sept-place* will be the
fastest way to go.

"Three hours to the border, but then, the road…" He
trails off and gestures with his hand. "I don't know."

"Is there another route to Boké?"

"Labé," he says. "There are two border crossings. The
faster route, it's Quebo. But commerce takes the other
route."

We are in heavy traffic, crawling up the busy market street in Bissau, traffic crowding us on either side. When we find ourselves nearly stationary, a police officer strides up to the open driver's side window. Our driver reaches up to the sun visor and produces what appears to be his licence. The officer nods and waves us onward.

"They want money," he says. "This is Guinea Bissau. But if your documents are in order, it's okay. But you should know that when you get to Guinea, there will be fees along the way."

IT'S A MAN'S WORLD AT THE TRANSIT PARK. ONE MAN LINGERS in front of his two-wheeled Nescafé cart and cools his steaming coffee by pouring it back and forth between two tiny plastic cups. Vendors mill around him, hawking sunglasses and imitation gold chains. If you had all the time in the world, you could wait in this dusty parking lot all day. The vans are in no hurry. They only leave when they are full, and they are full only rarely.

We don't have all day, so we buy seven of the eight seats in the closest van, which is something that only wealthy Westerners can do. The eighth seat is purchased by a mother carrying her infant child in her lap, and the two of them occupy the front seat. The window of our van is made of meticulously applied transparent tape. If you weren't paying close attention, you might even foolishly believe it was glass.

It costs three thousand francs for passage to the border town of Kunta Bano, another name that only exists on a map. We're on our own from there, since nothing with four wheels can continue the journey beyond that point.

"*Só moto*," says the van driver some three hours later when we arrive unceremoniously at the end of the sealed road. Only motorcycles.

The nursing woman exits the van with her child and points us in the direction of two men standing idle next to a roadside hut. We approach them on foot, all our worldly belongings slung across our backs. It's unclear what is supposed to happen next – only that getting to Guinea by land was never meant to be easy.

The moto drivers look about twenty years old, give or take five years.

One wears a floral print shirt, loose soccer pants, and has his phone tucked over his ear, squashed into submission beneath his helmet. He greets us and calls himself Morano. His partner wears a shirt that reads POLICIA, although he is clearly not the police and never has been. He doesn't call himself anything and prefers to let Morano do the talking.

It's around noon and having settled on an acceptable price to reach Boké, everything seems to unfolding according to plan. It could still be a bad plan, but everything is unfolding according to it. Melody rides with Morano, and

I ride with the other, who has now hidden his POLICIA shirt underneath a red jacket. We don't receive helmets, but it's a frivolous complaint under the circumstances.

The dirt road to the Guinea Bissau border is always bumpy, often monotonous, but intermittently beautiful. Africa is both vast and hauntingly empty. Through my increasingly translucent sunglasses, the dust and dirt glow deep mahogany red. Occasionally, we pass traditional thatched huts and other village homes constructed with adobe bricks. Women wash their clothes in shallow streams and walk beside the trails with plastic buckets balanced skillfully atop their heads. In the fields, the locals are working hard – chopping, picking, digging, carrying, cleaning. Within the towns and villages, they are hardly working. Instead, they sprawl lethargically in all manner of broken plastic chairs, watching dust swirl around them as the world passes them by.

Before long, we have arrived at what appears to be the border post, a hut with an open window to receive us. Two women copy our passport information into a ledger. Then, an old man wearing army fatigues leads us into a neighbouring hut. He only has one seeing eye, the other eye opaque and white with a ripe cataract. The hut smells strongly of onions.

He gestures for us to show him the inside of our bags, but when we unzip them and obediently push them towards him, he makes no move to peer inside. Instead, his gaze rests on the two of us as he smiles warmly.

"*Je suis très heureux*," he finally says. He is very happy. We smile back.

"*Enchanté*," Melody says to him as we leave his hut. The French certainly have a way with words. We return to our motorcycles, thoroughly enchanted with this charming old man.

AS IT TURNS OUT, OUR ENCOUNTER WITH THE ONE-EYED old man did not represent the end of Guinea Bissau-Guinea border formalities. We travel another thirty minutes by motorcycle until we reach a small clearing in the wilderness. Here, we find a large, thatched gazebo and several smaller huts nearby.

A uniformed Bissau Guinean officer invites us into the gazebo, where he copies our passport information into another ledger. His wife sits alongside, quietly peeling an onion. When the officer has finished, he invites us to exchange money with him. It occurs to me that being asked by an armed border agent to change money with him cannot stray far from the textbook definition of conflict of interest, but this might not be the time for self-righteous grandstanding.

"I think you should exchange ten thousand francs," he suggests.

I thank him for his generous offer and agree that ten thousand francs happens to be precisely the amount I had hoped to exchange. I'm equally certain that whatever exchange rate he offers will be more than fair. Reluctantly, I hand over a small stack of bills and wait as he counts out the corresponding stack of Guinean francs. As we leave his hut, he inspects Melody from head to toe without any particular subtlety.

"Japanese?" he suggests.

Taiwanese, strictly speaking.

"Very close!" I interject, just in case Melody had been considering contradicting him. Instead, she nods in agreement. "Very close."

Melody consults the currency calculator on her phone. Astonishingly, his exchange rate was fair. It seems the officer was only trying to be helpful. Having finished with us, he points across the clearing towards the next hut. This one is considerably smaller, and proportionately darker inside.

A youthful soldier beckons. He's wire thin, almost to the point of emaciation. I look down at his feet and note that he is wearing standard issue army boots. I was told once that any ambitious paramilitary revolutionary with a dream can cover himself in army camouflage, but that only a legitimate soldier wears real army boots. I don't know if it's true, but it struck me as something that *could* be true.

His desk is little more than a splintered wooden crate. He copies our passport information into another identical ledger and then looks up bashfully, almost apologetically.

"Give one thousand francs. Two, if you can. *Troca.*"

I don't harbour any ill will against him, so I split the difference and give him one thousand five hundred francs. He seems like a pleasant young man, and he extorts me like a perfect gentleman.

FOR THE NEXT LEG OF THE VOYAGE, MORANO AND HIS friend secure our backpacks to the rear of their motor- cycles with twine, and then cover them with a plastic tarp. We continue onward. Unexpectedly, the bush trail leads at least an hour deeper into the jungle as we push steadily toward the Guinea Bissau-Guinea border.

As we travel, the path gradually narrows until it is no wider than a well-marked hiking trail, space perhaps for three villagers to walk abreast. Here, Melody and Morano fall behind, gradually at first, and then lost without a trace beyond the curves of the winding trail. The previously un- mistakeable hum of their motorcycle grows increasingly faint until it is inaudible. My own driver silently carries us onward into the bush for what seems an eternity. We don't pass any other villagers. I begin to doubt whether I will ever see Melody again.

"*Onde sao os outros?*" I ask my driver hesitantly, over

the sound of our own motorcycle. My Portuguese is limited to the survival variety. *Where are the others?*

He doesn't answer. I try again.

"*Où sont les autres?*"

No answer.

I briefly wonder if this is where we will be robbed and murdered. On some level, I suppose that as her male traveling companion, I am expected to fill the hero role, defending Melody from those who would do her harm. That means that if Morano has stopped to murder Melody, then I will certainly also be killed. One cannot happen without the other. There's no sense leaving behind a lone dissatisfied customer.

But if they don't do so now, then it liberates us to place perfect trust in our drivers. Because why would they go to the trouble of shepherding us safely through this hazardous and uninhabited terrain, only to rob and murder us at the last possible moment?

When we arrive at the border, there is a rope obstructing the trail ahead. Shreds of plastic grocery bags are tied to the rope at equal intervals to make it more visible against the encroaching wilderness. Behind this makeshift checkpoint lies a small concrete building with a service window. My driver points toward the structure.

"*Documentos,*" he says.

I point behind us to suggest we should wait for Melody

and Morano, and this time he seems to understand. At first, there is a long silence. Then, the crescendo hum of a distant motor, before the two finally appear amid the trees and dense brush, gliding closer and closer until the bike comes to rest beside us.

"I thought you were dead," I say to Melody.

"I thought so too," says Melody.

Inside the service window sits a large, perfectly round face attached to a pudgy neck. The pudgy man silently copies our passport information into another large ledger, then looks up at me. His voice is an impossibly deep, commanding baritone.

"Give twenty thousand. Gate fee."

It seems expensive, about thirty dollars, especially considering that gate is really just a rope with plastic bags tied to it. It couldn't possibly cost thirty dollars to lower it.

"Can we just give ten thousand?" I ask him, doubtfully. He shakes his head.

Morano steps in and points out that he is referring to Guinean francs, not the more valuable CFA francs used in Guinea Bissau. The amount the official is asking for comes to about two dollars. He should have taken my first offer. As a bribe, it's more than fair.

I CONSULT THE MAP SAVED ON MY PHONE, AND OUR LOCA-tion appears as a blue dot nestled within the vast emptiness just inside the Guinean border. If it were not for satellites in space, we would be hopelessly lost. Maybe even the satellites don't make much difference. Morano and his friend are our only salvation in this jungle, and our lives are in their hands. We still don't have an entry stamp on our passports, which means that as far as anyone is concerned, we could be illegal migrants slipping into Guinea undetected.

Up ahead, Morano stops his bike and cuts the motor. My driver pulls up beside him and does the same. He leans forward over his handlebars, frowning. The forest around us is dense, silent, and empty.

"Now, you show me your money."

"What?"

"You must show me your money."

"Why?"

I cautiously extract my wallet, filled with a mix of Guinean francs and those from Guinea Bissau. No use fighting this. I hand him a few large Guinean bills, hoping it will be enough to keep this harrowing adventure going. If he wants more – if he wants all of it – we'll know soon enough.

Morano takes my money, sorts through it, then slowly hands it back to me, separating a twenty thousand franc note from the others. Then, he hands that note back to me as well.

"Never have more than this."

I look back at him blankly.

"I think he wants you to keep twenty thousand francs in your pocket all the time," exclaims Melody, as if she has solved a complex riddle.

Yes. That could be it.

I push the note down into the pocket of my filthy hiking pants. Morano fires up his motor.

WHEN I WAS A CHILD, I READ *THE LITTLE PRINCE*, WHICH IS now one of the most translated books ever published. In its pages, the titular character leaves the asteroid that he once called home in order to visit various planets in space (and their curious inhabitants) before finally arriving on Earth. In the remote wilds of the Guinean jungle, we too visit many planets along with their curious inhabitants. In practice, every dusty intersection in Guinea has its own *roi du carrefour*. I'm not sure who empowers them, how much power they have, or why.

On the first planet, we encounter a group of three soldiers in repose underneath a shady tree. Each of the soldiers is dressed slightly differently, but all are wearing army boots. Morano and his friend glide up next to them on their bikes and the soldiers command us to dismount.

Passport. Visa. Yellow fever card.

I extract my copy from the pocket of my backpack. The photocopy has nearly disintegrated in the humidity.

The first soldier wants to know where he can find the expiry date on my yellow fever card, and I point out the faded date stamp.

"Where is the original?" demands the second soldier.

"It's in my bag somewhere."

"She is not Canadian," says the second soldier, pointing to Melody. "Where is she from?"

"Canada," says Melody stubbornly.

"Why are you in Guinea?" says the third soldier. His voice is softer. He seems genuinely interested.

"Tourism."

"Just tourism?" says the third soldier.

"Guinea is beautiful?" interjects the second soldier. It seems to be a question. He glances over at the third soldier.

"Yes, I suppose so," says the third soldier.

"Give ten thousand," says the first soldier.

I give him ten thousand francs.

ON THE SECOND PLANET, THE TRAIL IS OBSTRUCTED BY ANother rope with shreds of plastic bags tied to it. We are directed to dismount our bikes, and a man directs us uphill towards a small hut, where we find a well-fed man ensconced behind his desk. I cannot see his boots.

Passport. Visa. Yellow fever card.

"What is in the bags on the moto?" he demands.

"Clothes, medicine."

"Show me." He gestures down the hill, unsmiling and severe. I hesitate, because our bags have been so meticulously secured to our motorbikes that it will take forever just to remove them, let alone search them, if that is indeed what this man plans to do. We could be here all afternoon. I suspect he knows this.

We descend the hill to find Morano and his friend waiting for us patiently.

"Uh, he wants to see inside the bags," I tell Morano.

Morano throws his hands up. He seems irritated, exasperated by our infantile naivete and confusion.

"Just give ten thousand!"

With that, he marches us back up the hill and into the hut. He stands behind us like a parent who has escorted his reluctant child to the neighbour's house to supervise a forced apology. I give the fat man ten thousand francs.

"Always have only twenty thousand ready in your pocket," Morano scolds me when we are done. I nod.

ON THE THIRD PLANET, WE FIND A SOLITARY MAN WEARING a felt hat and black army fatigues. His hut is darker and moodier than the others. He is potbellied, and his bare feet are propped on the wooden table in front of him. He drags on his cigarette as we walk in, the archetype of every tinpot dictator who has ever graced a Hollywood screen. A rifle hangs from its strap on the wall behind him. There's no question in my mind that this petty man is not the keeper of the entry stamp that we're looking for.

He wants ten thousand.

The shakedowns are arriving at the rate of about a dollar fifty per person. They are not so much bribes as they are extortion at the hands of insignificant men invested with questionable degrees of power. A bribe implies that we have somehow done something wrong, which we are now desperately attempting to rectify. But we've done nothing wrong except exist in Guinea as naïve and artless foreigners. How much, then, should our integrity be worth?

I briefly consider this question and decide that today, the market price is one dollar and fifty cents. In other words, I give ten thousand francs.

The jungle is at its most dense when we reach the river crossing, and we are startled to see the silhouettes of several men lurking in the shadows among the trees as we approach. Morano and his friend do not seem remotely alarmed, and that sets our own minds at ease. We trust the men lurking in the bushes by association.

Our motorcycles pull up beside them and we dismount while our drivers negotiate the terms of our passage. We are baffled, since the river seems to span at least a half kilometre and there is no ferry in sight.

Morano leads us down the riverbank to a rickety wooden pirogue, constructed with roughly hewn planks of bare plywood crisscrossed at the bow and stern with more splintered boards that serve as seats. For the modest price of twenty-five thousand francs, our drivers have no reservations about wheeling their heavy motorcycles onto this narrow canoe, one by one lengthwise, alongside our backpacks. This too, is reassuring since it means they trust this contraption enough to risk their lives and livelihoods on its questionable seaworthiness.

Five of us board the boat – five too many as far as I am concerned – and it rocks slightly under our collective weight. I shift my body to one side in an attempt to counterbalance the canoe. There are no lifejackets, but no turning back now. Capsizing would be catastrophic, first for the motorcycles, second for our luggage, and for us as a distant third. At least for the human cargo, there would remain some chance of rescue, since I estimate that with some effort, I could flail back to shore, barring any interference from roaming crocodiles.

The boatman paddles slowly across the calm water, the canoe still listing gently from side to side. The treacherous crossing lasts only a few minutes, after which the pirogue lurches to rest in the dirt and mud of the opposing riverbank. We scramble away from the boat like frightened schoolchildren carrying our backpacks, even before the two motorcycles have been unloaded.

Then, scarce moments later, Morano and his partner

invite us to mount the bikes again, all without a word of consolation for the harrowing and emotionally traumatic experience we have just lived through. Perhaps they make this crossing every afternoon.

Ahead of us, the bridge is out. That's an understatement. The bridge has an enormous and irregular hole through its floor, the sort created when someone tries to rest a marble on top a piece of wet tissue paper. In this case, that marble might have been some unfortunate truck, in too much of a hurry to take the less direct (but more paved) route through Labé.

But it's dry season, and Morano quickly finds a detour through a stream that is presently only knee-deep. My own driver follows him into the water, stalls briefly mid-crossing, walks our bike through, and then guns the motor when he reaches the other side. The next bridge has a similar defect, but this one is covered in a bed of rebar, perhaps to allow determined pedestrians and tightrope walkers to pass. My shoes have only just dried from the previous detour when another cool current washes over my ankles.

The deep crescendo of another motor grows ahead of us, and we pull our motorcycles over amongst the trees. A truck appears along the path, rumbling towards us like a tank, sprawling across the impossibly narrow jungle trail, and belching an opaque cloud of grey dust and exhaust behind him. A sign draped over the front fender reads *Bonne*

Chance, which is a little on the nose. His existence here is ridiculous. He must be heading towards the border with Guinea Bissau.

"How does he plan to cross those bridges?" I ask Melody while we are stopped.

"Or the river?" She shrugs. "*Bonne chance*, I guess."

THE FOURTH AND FINAL PLANET HOSTS AN AIRY, THATCHED hut and has a rope that obstructs its intersection with what my map ambitiously refers to as the *N3 highway*. In reality, it is merely a turnoff from one dirt road onto another, more spacious dirt road. By now, dismounting the bike and preparing ten thousand francs has become old hat.

The man inside this hut has a puffy, kind face, and when we enter his abode, he is sucking on a lime. He greets us with a warm smile.

"Hello. Would you like a lime?" he asks Melody when she approaches, documents in hand.

"No, thank you." Melody smiles back at him, and he flips through our passports. To my amazement, I notice a wooden stamp and an inkpad next to his right hand. This is it.

The puffy man inspects her paper visa.

"Most people come in with the page open, and the visa is already in the passport. So now, I don't know where to stamp!"

He seems genuinely bewildered. Melody leans over his wooden counter and flips her passport to one of its many remaining blank pages.

"Maybe you can stamp it right here?" she gently suggests, pointing to the empty page while flashing a mischievous grin. I think she is flirting with him. If she plays her cards right, soon he will inquire as to whether she is Japanese or Chinese.

"Oh! Yes."

I assume this remote jungle outpost isn't a common border for Westerners to cross. This man must spend most of his lonely days sitting, waiting, and sucking on limes. Moments later he confirms my suspicions.

"We don't get too many Canadians. Maybe one or two a year." He combs through his dusty ledger, searching through scribbled names and assorted nationalities with a chubby finger. "The last Canadian was January 18. You are the second and third this year."

He stamps our passports. He smiles again and wishes us safe travels, although his goodwill is mostly directed toward Melody. We then make our way back to Morano and his friend. Something is missing, and it strikes me as very strange.

I still have ten thousand francs in my pocket.

THE N3 HIGHWAY MIGHT BE A DIRT ROAD, BUT IT IS COM-
fortably wide and flanked by only scarce trees, giving it a
sense of openness that we haven't encountered before. There
are roadside stands, and even the occasional enclosed structure. The feeling of acceleration, and the wind in my face
gives this leg of the journey a greater sense of movement
than before. My hair is rigid and matted with dust, and
my skin is caked in a film that makes it difficult to smile.
But those are minor complaints, because it's now late in the
afternoon, the sun is low, and we're nearly in Boké.

Before we arrive, there is another hut beside the road.
Another demand to dismount. Another two men inside
the hut.

One wears a US Marines uniform, and he sits cross-
legged on a soiled and bare mattress with his back leaning
against the wall of the hut. The other is a man dressed
in light blue, and I can't immediately distinguish whether
they are blue army fatigues or blue hospital scrubs. He is
very dark, very severe, and very much barefoot. His calloused feet rest comfortably upon a plastic chair. No boots.

The two would-be soldiers pass our passports back and
forth and appear to pore over them in excruciating detail,
inspecting each page line by line. The barefoot man seems
to be the one in charge, and he is doing his best to come
across as intimidating. But there is something comical
about him, this hut, this journey, and suddenly, it's all I

can do not to burst into laughter. *Do the line*, I think to myself.

"Give twenty thousand."

"Twenty thousand?" I say incredulously. "For both of us?"

"Each."

It's steep. Perhaps the rent is higher on these main roads. But more likely they are just greedy. I reach into my wallet and Morano is already behind me to provide moral support. "Just give twenty thousand."

That's what I do, and the would-be soldiers take the banknote handed to them without rebuttal. If we had known just how impotent these benignly corrupt officials were from the start, it's possible we could have saved upwards of six dollars.

We're on the outskirts of our destination by five-thirty, and Morano stops at a roadside garage because his bike needs something tightened. As we open our plastic bottles to gulp what remains of our warm water, Morano turns to us.

"Where do you stay in Boké?"

I look over to Melody, who is unrecognizable, her skin nearly the same colour as the dirt beside the road, and her eyelids thick with dust. Only one word occurs to me. *Sanctuary*.

"What's the best hotel in town?"

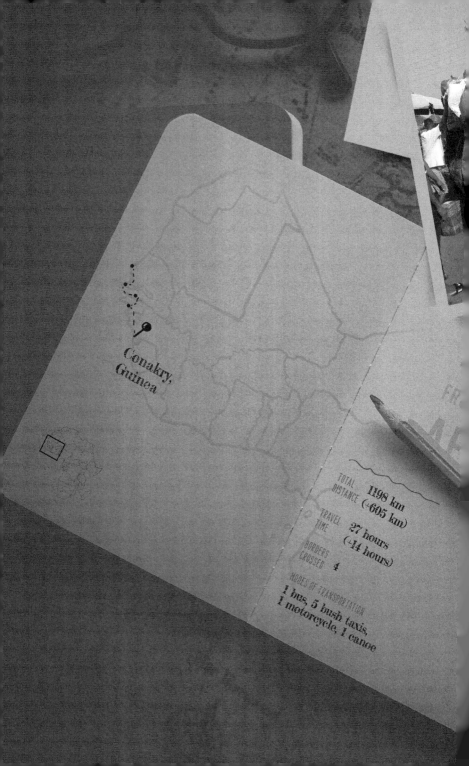

Conakry,
Guinea

TOTAL 1198 km
DISTANCE (~605 km)

TRAVEL 27 hours
TIME (~14 hours)

BORDERS 4
CROSSED

MODES OF TRANSPORTATION
1 bus, 5 bush taxis,
1 motorcycle, 1 canoe

Guinea writ large is the purest example of entropy that most are likely to encounter – from its rugged landscape to its chaotic towns and cities – and that could be seen as part of its appeal. Then again, maybe not. Few travelers make it to Guinea. Fewer still make the long land journey from Conakry to Freetown, but if you do, this is how it might look – bush taxi and all. This short story is intended to be a fast-paced adventure tale, and one as likely as the last to terrify my mother.

NOTES ON A RENAULT 19

THE AFRICAN SUN IS EXHAUSTING. STRICTLY SPEAKING, IT must be the same sun as everywhere else on the planet, but somehow this one is more blinding, more oppressive, and from it there can be no escape. The car itself is a greenhouse, making it imperative for the window to remain open, no matter how noxious the polluted air outside. For these and other reasons, Melody despises Guinea, but I disagree. Guinea is an adventure, and I'm confident that its charms will win her over.

"*Beaucoup beaucoup beaucoup beaucoup de camions chinois!*" announces our driver, gesturing towards the passing convoy of lumbering trucks on the remaining highway between Boké and Conakry. "There is bauxite in there."

The trucks are cinnamon coloured with dust. They are so thoroughly brown that not a single remnant of their original colour remains. They are brown from the cab, to the tires, all the way up to the fluttering tarp that blankets their cargo. The dust mingles with the exhaust fumes to produce a hazy fog that rises up above and behind the vehicles.

"Legislative elections come soon," he says. "Then, the presidential election. Our president has been president for ten years. But he is not a good president."

"Why not?"

"He doesn't pay the truck drivers! Have you seen all these trucks? The Chinese sent money to pay the truck drivers, but the president does not pay them. They move all this bauxite without being paid."

He looks over at Melody, seeming to register that she could very well be Chinese. Or perhaps Japanese.

"The Chinese are not so bad," he concedes. "The investment is good for improving poverty. The Guineans work for the Chinese on credit. But the Chinese are blind! The Chinese, they give twelve million, but the government only pays the drivers four million. It is not the Chinese who are the problem. It is the Guineans! The Chinese paid!"

Our policy is to never interrupt a local mid-rant, and so we nod gamely and allow him to continue.

"Guineans are thieves!" he says, raising his voice in pitch as much as volume. "The president, too, he is a thief. He wants to change the constitution for a third mandate.

If he does that, it is not good. The government of Guinea, it is not good. And the president, he grew up in France. He is not even a real Guinean!"

The excitable driver is an old friend of Morano's. Once in a while he leans out the window to shout something in French at a passing car or truck. The traffic intensifies. We've reached the outskirts of Conakry.

"Me, I live in Conakry," he says. "Many people in Conakry."

It certainly seems that way. The highway median leading into the city is piled high with bags of garbage. The occasional rainwater puddles seem to fluoresce with the bright green of nuclear waste and smell worse. It's dry season. I can only imagine that rainy season would turn the streets into murky swampland.

In the shantytowns surrounding the city, the locals noisily go about their business. Women dry their clothes in the gutter, sharing the road with brightly painted Renaults, yellow with stripes. At the intersections, messy accumulations of food stalls and umbrellas. Looming above the metropolis, the Chinese have built a concrete monstrosity, a monolithic skyscraper called the Hotel Kakimbo which rises from the nothingness of the outskirts of the city. It is their sanctuary, their home away from home in Guinea.

In Guinea, a sanctuary is needed more than anywhere else, because the social contract is broken. In Conakry, everything is either urgent or desperate, and nothing can wait. There is scarcely room to breathe.

As we make our way to the bus station, we pass over a bridge just as a woman walks to its railing to shotput a bag of garbage into the ocean. Beside her, another man is urinating into the water. I assume that her trash disposal was urgent, and that the urinating man simply couldn't wait. But it is the traffic that is completely impossible.

Just ahead, a truck has parked in the middle of the highway, leaving only the opposing lane free. Why it has chosen to stop there is impossible to say. What is clear is that no one will stop to allow the opposing traffic through. Only a trickle of motorcycles can slip past, all while an impressive gridlock of larger four wheeled vehicles piles up behind us. There is a police officer wandering aimlessly up ahead, because in Guinea, there is nearly always at least one uniformed officer within view. This would have represented a perfect opportunity for him to do some useful work.

Our driver loses his patience and buts his car into the mess anyway. The fare we're paying him is fixed, so time is money and everything is urgent. He leans out the window to yell at the oncoming driver. She screams back at him. She's upset (somewhat understandably) not because even those few motorcycles can no longer pass through – but because *she* cannot pass through.

The chorus of horns behind us grows louder. The pungent Conakry air is stagnant outside our window. Melody would claim this is why she despises Guinea. The social contract is broken.

WE FIND OURSELVES IN ANOTHER TRANSIT PARK, THIS ONE larger than the others. It might resemble the vast terminal of a busy airport, if only that terminal were open to the searing white sky, paved entirely with asphalt, congested with a mayhem of hundreds of cars and trucks, and crowded with thousands of Guineans.

Our driver deposits us near an agent selling tickets for Freetown. He is a man perched upon six stacked plastic chairs, with a large wooden table in front of him. The more chairs, the more power. Some of the less powerful men around him sit on bags of rice, occasionally glancing over at us apathetically.

I ask for two seats, in French. He answers me, in English. I ask him what time the car will leave, in French.

"You can't just change back and forth between French and English," he says, again in English. Then he obliges, accepts my Guinean francs, and begins to scribble on two paper ticket stubs.

"What is the name of the woman?"

The agent waves vaguely in Melody's direction but does not turn his head. He has enormous hands and a deeply resonant voice. His eye contact is unwavering, or at least it is with me. In West Africa, Melody experiences one of two reactions, each in approximately equal measure. The first is complete engagement, as if each man who interacts with her is fully committed to a courtship ritual in which my presence causes some unspoken resentment. They want to know where she is from, where she has been, what she does, and what she likes about their country, usually while closely inspecting her from head to toe. They would sniff her if they could. She responds to this treatment with *bouncer voice*, best described as the voice that a young woman uses when trying to convince a steroid-enhanced bouncer to allow her and six well-dressed friends into his nightclub.

This is the second reaction – complete indifference, presumably because when it comes to money, the decision-making capacity must certainly rest with the man. Melody prefers the first reaction, while I am partial to the second.

"Is this your wife?" says the agent, his body angled away from her.

"Yes," I say, because it will make matters less complicated.

"What is the phone number of the woman?"

I don't know, and since I'm not sure what difference it will make, I give him my own.

At the other end of the wooden table, lunch arrives, a single heaping serving of *riz gras* poured into a large wash-basin. Six men use separate forks to consume its contents. Between them, the rice disappears within a minute, as does the basin.

All across the parking lot, Guineans sit atop ramshackle vehicles stacked so high with boxes of goods that they look like souvenir cars. The centre of gravity of each is some-where well above the roof. The boxes have been rendered indestructible, sealed from the elements with packing tape wound tightly a thousand times over.

"Africa," says a smiling man walking by, pointing to the improbable stack of boxes balanced upon our own bush taxi. A local is hurrying to cover the cargo with a black tarp. "*C'est comme ça!*"

We laugh. Africa certainly is *like this*, and Guinea more like this than anywhere else. I point out to Melody that people travel from across the world to witness the changing of the guard at Buckingham Palace, the famous souks of Morocco, the bright lights and hypermodernity of Tokyo simply because some travel writer has convinced them that those things are the *main event*. But the main event in Guinea is this mayhem – this filthy transit park in which the locals build Jenga towers of merchandise atop cars that anywhere else would have been chopped up for parts long ago. It's performance art. This country can be often infuriating, but never boring. It's all a matter of perspective and maintaining the proper mindset. Guinea is the victory of rugged individualism.

We wait on a bench and stare out at the transit park, admiring the show.

Beside us, an old man with a craggy face and the snowy wisps of a scant goatee is trying to sell his prayer mats, emerald green and blue with gold tassels. The salesman who follows is a walking pharmacy with a bucket perched on his head filled with tiny boxes of medicine. The man sitting beside us has no interest in the prayer mats but instead buys a small box of medicine from the walking pharmacy. The medicine seems to be a type of natural aphrodisiac, if the well-endowed woman pictured on the front of the box is any indication.

The man stares at it intently. He seems very pleased with his purchase. He is still staring at the box when the ticket agent beckons us to our vehicle. Apparently, we will be leaving for Freetown momentarily.

On my side of this Renault 19, the driver uses a wrench to wind down the window, the handle presumably a long-forgotten memory from this vehicle's youth. Somewhere, once upon a time, this automobile emerged from a factory, or rolled out of a dealership, freshly waxed and brand new. That time was thirty long years ago, in 1989, when the Renault 19 was awarded Car of the Year in Spain and Germany.

But today, this is a vehicle with negative value, as the economists would say. That is, if someone left it parked on your front lawn with the keys still in the ignition, you would chase that person down the street and demand he pay you to have it towed to the scrapyard. You would haul him by his shirt back to your lawn, point furiously to the peeling paint, irregular scratches, and deep dents that mark the outer hull of the car. You would point out that there is nothing left of the inner doors but bare metal and rust. That the windshield is badly cracked. That the cushions on the seats are tattered and stained. Get this car off my lawn, you would demand, or I'm calling the police.

But Guinea has plenty of use for this and other similar Renaults, which serve as the country's mules, hustling both people and goods across or out of the country.

When all passengers are finally packed inside, we are three in the front, two in the middle, and two in the back – the two in the back are a man and a woman who are speaking neither English nor French. My head brushes against the roof of this wreck, which appears to be on the verge of caving in from the massive weight of its overhead cargo. It is like there is an elephant asleep on the roof of the car.

Back on Melody's side, the driver slams the door a half dozen times. There is an obnoxious *thump* each time the door collides with the body of the car. In the end, the door won't stay closed and instead sags limply from its hinges as if thoroughly exhausted by the effort.

By eleven o'clock, the driver has tied the passenger door closed with a rope that wraps around the underside of the car like twine around a bundle of sticks. Perhaps this door once closed properly but doesn't close today. Perhaps it never closed, and the rope trick is one he's used for years. Either way, it's not a car that is roadworthy. It's a car that should be condemned, of little use even for its component parts.

But not today. Today this Renault 19 bush taxi is all that stands between us and Freetown.

As we pull out from the lot, the boys who loaded the cargo onto the roof are banging on the hood and shouting. Seems our driver either didn't pay them at all or didn't pay them enough. Guinea. *C'est comme ça*. The disorder, the urgency, and the palpable rumble of panic that underlies even the most banal of daily routines.

TWENTY MINUTES LATER, WE STOP ON AN UNPAVED SIDE street for urgent door repairs. A mechanic emerges from a doorway and tinkers on Melody's side of the car with a wrench. On my side, I watch an adolescent boy wander down the dirt road. He is wearing a United States Army uniform, but it is about fifteen sizes too large and reaches below his knees. Behind us, the two passengers in the back seat are clucking their tongues and sucking their teeth in disapproval. They aren't happy about this delay.

"Where are you two from?" asks Melody.

"We come from Sierra Leone," says the woman in the back seat, in heavily accented English. "And you?"

"Canada," says Melody. There might be nothing more unifying than the mutual annoyance of strangers faced with a common irritation. Several dozen dull thuds, squeaks, and taps later and the passenger door closes and miraculously remains closed. The mechanic scampers away. Then, finally, we're back on the highway, leaving the chaos of Conakry behind.

At the intermittent bribe checkpoints, it seems the standard protocol is that we provide either identification, or failing that, ten thousand Guinean francs. We're unfazed by this, now well-acquainted with the knowledge that Guinea is *comme ça*.

"The police checkpoints are to guard the villages, because there are bandits," explains the driver. "There are military too. They're everywhere for the security of the population."

At three o'clock, we pop a flat tire. Our speed gradually slows, and the driver seems to be having increasing difficulty keeping the car in a straight line. We stop beside the road in a small village and rest in a shady field while he changes the tire. We note that the tire is so flat by the time we stop, and the wheel well so misshapen, that he must have been driving on it for hours. And although it takes longer to appreciate the aesthetics, my vantage point from this grassy field allows me to note that our battered Renault is a unique and remarkable piece of accidental art. The yellow racing stripe on the hood leading down to the peeling decal of eagle's wings. The four shades of faded blue paint, one melting imperceptibly into the next, until that abrupt transition to the fiery red of the rear of the car. Most of all, the scratches, the rust, and the shattered headlights and taillights. There will never be a car quite like it, nor should there be.

Our driver rolls the spent tire into the ditch beside the road, where it will one day become a treasure for someone else to find. We climb back inside and set off again towards the border.

The roads are worn away at the edges, as if termites have nibbled away at them, and the car swerves frequently to skirt the largest of the many potholes. As often as not, the highway is unpaved, and the Renault kicks up tornadoes of dust as it meanders through the dirt and rocks. A haze approaching us means oncoming traffic, and both vehicles then slow to pass each other along the single narrow lane.

A certain rhythm of creaking and moaning becomes familiar as the car careens erratically along the highway.

The goods on (and in) the car are clearly worth more than the car itself, and our driver knows it. The Renault exists only as a means to transport cargo from one capital city to the next. The Salones in the back seat aren't happy about the delays.

"Sierra Leone is not like this," the Salone woman says to us, smiling. "Only Guinea is like this."

Plenty of daylight remains, but the border is inexplicably closed when we reach Parmelap by late afternoon. Our driver pulls over and waves us out of the vehicle. We stand patiently under the awning of a general store, where a villager sells us two hard boiled eggs and a banana. The driver passes the time by changing another tire. The sky, at first washed out and white with the full brilliance of the sun, gradually becomes muted as the shadows of passing pedestrians lengthen. We peel the eggs and the banana while sitting cross-legged on the patio of the store and looking out at the growing queue of parked Renaults and motorcycles.

"For enough money, however," suggests one of the Salones helpfully, "the border is always open."

If only that were true. What's more, there are no real restaurants nor hotels in Parmelap, and it's not the sort of border town that welcomes visitors. Across the road, a bright blue and yellow sign above a blue door reads *Bienvenu au What's App Bar*, but the door is padlocked and there are no signs of life on its dusty patio. Our driver could leave us here in Parmelap to fend for ourselves, but I doubt it. It's more likely, argues my eternal optimist, that when night finally descends, he will help us find an inexpensive *African standard* room in which to hole up until morning.

But border towns are never safe. The locals will know we are tourists, that we therefore have money and expensive electronics, and that we won't be hard to find. I envision a twin bed housed in a run-down apartment complex, the room dimly lit by a single bulb hanging from a wire. We will take shifts standing vigil beside the door or peering out the window into the near-total darkness of the street, scanning for suspicious movements. I will eventually let my guard down, drift into a quiet slumber, only to be awoken by the inevitable thump of footsteps on the hallway landing, followed by the scratching of a key inside the lock.

Perhaps the Salones will help us. There's safety in numbers.

"What's your anxiety level right now, from one to ten?" I ask Melody.

"Eight," she answers. She has been quiet since we arrived in Parmelap, possibly because she is in the midst of an internal meltdown.

"I'm running at about a seven right now," I say truthfully. "But maybe we still have time to head back to Conakry. I wonder what the highway bandit situation is like at night."

"Don't even joke about that."

I'm not sure whether she is more frightened of the bandits, or Conakry itself.

The distant fringes of the sky are tinged with orange. It won't be long now before the trap is set, and Guinea seals us inside its borders for another night. No one is coming to save us. Nothing more can be done, and there is a certain element of relief in this helplessness – this powerless resignation to whatever plans the universe has in store for this journey towards Freetown.

Just then, there is a crescendo clamour of restless sounds, a low murmur of conversation punctuated by staccato shouts. Passengers hastily gathering their belongings and scrambling towards the lineup of battered automobiles. Then, the sound of dozens of motors simultaneously firing and Renaults limping from the ditch back onto the main road that leads to Freetown and freedom.

"Driver!" I shout, waving my arms wildly. The Salones do the same, pacing up and down the road to look for him. He saunters out from one of the shops on the strip, then breaks into a brisk trot when we catch his eye. Cars continue to pass us on the single lane highway. It's an old-fashioned run on the border gates, and those gates will close at six o'clock, trapping us inside Guinea. We pile into the car, and our driver fires up the ignition. He wants this border crossing as badly as we do, because in Guinea, everything is urgent and nothing can wait.

The border is anarchy, a commotion of agents shouting in French as dozens of vehicles attempt to sneak through the checkpoint at all costs. Traffic has jammed the road itself, so the cars have instead splayed themselves at odd angles across the dirt and sparse grass of the clearing, jockeying for space. An agent armed with a pistol dashes up to my passenger-side window. He is unhappy with our driver's audacious attempt to squeeze through.

"*Descend! Descend!*" He pounds his fist against my door, demanding that I get out. I'd like to, but when I try to open the door, I cannot. The latch is stuck, and I assume it probably requires a wrench and some aggressive jiggling. But the agent is a Guinean. He must be well aware that sometimes doors just don't open, just as sometimes they don't close. Meanwhile, our driver's dogged attempts to weave through the tangle of cars are finally frustrated, and he leans forward on the steering wheel in resignation.

WE'RE FORCED TO WALK THE REMAINING DISTANCE TO THE Guinean customs post. At the first checkpoint, I can't find my yellow fever vaccination card, and two customs agents wait with greedy anticipation as I frantically dig through the pockets of my backpack.

"We should take him inside," suggests the first agent. The other waves him off and lets me pass. It's a surprising reversal of fortunes.

"Don't worry, I paid your bribe," says Melody as we continue onward.

"Thanks. I owe you one."

The main customs building is a sizable structure, and we follow a loosely connected crowd into a tiny office where another uniformed Guinean agent takes our passports. Guineans and foreigners alike have forced themselves through the door of the office, and it isn't entirely clear if we are a queue or simply a huddled and hopeful mass. One thing is clear. In situations like this, one should always, *always* keep a watchful eye on one's passport.

The officer disappears into a back room, and I watch the door swing closed behind him. He re-emerges. Our passports are still tucked inside his right hand. He races past us and vanishes down a dark corridor. We instinctively chase after him, around a bend and into a second, larger room. But something is missing. I feel light. I've forgotten my day pack on the floor of the first office. Panicked, I dash back down the corridor to find it. Backpack separation syndrome. Passport separation syndrome. For the better part of a minute, I am a Canadian in Guinea with neither a visa, nor a passport. My backpack is where I left it, vulnerable and unguarded at the feet of an oblivious group of strangers. Then, having retrieved it with barely contained relief, I retrace my steps through the labyrinth of corridors and unmarked doors until I find Melody.

We are in a dark office, a half dozen chairs posed against the wall, a desk opposite us. An imposing Guinean official sits behind it, illuminating our documents under the beam of his flashlight. Several Asian tourists sit in one corner, and two Caucasians in the other. We wait to be processed in silent terror, a half dozen unruly children called into the principal's office for crimes yet unknown.

The principal picks up my passport and flips through it absentmindedly. Then he looks up at me.

"How did you like Guinea?" he says. His voice is a menacing baritone and his affect is flat. I'm caught off guard, because I don't want to lie, but I also don't want to offend. Those seem divergent goals.

"I liked it." I manage a forced smile.

"Be frank," scolds the principal, and then pauses to let the words sink in. "The people are very unfriendly. Guinea is very poor. I apologize for this."

I want to agree with him, but this could still be a trap. He's baiting me.

"Her and I have different opinions," I say, a rictus grin tensing my cheeks. I look over to Melody in an attempt to deflect his attention. "I thought Conakry was a very interesting city. The people are really nice! Really."

"Mmm." He seems satisfied. The interview is over and all that remains is one final bribe. Then, he stamps our exit and hands the passports back to us. With that, we thank him for his consideration and escape the room.

"I'm sorry I threw you under the bus," I tell Melody. "He was a little intimidating. And I couldn't exactly tell him that his country is the most entertaining one that I've ever been to."

"I think some of the nuance might have been lost in translation for sure," says Melody.

We find ourselves alone in a long corridor, bounded on one side by the various wings of the customs building, and on the other by a rope. We are still tense. For my part, I expect Guinean agents to leap out at any moment from either side to demand our visas, our yellow fever certificates, our passports. But instead, the next person to whom we hand our documents is an unassuming man poised behind a counter. He is all smiles, and he speaks in accented English.

"Melody," he reads from her documents. "Your name is pretty!"

"Thank you," says Melody.

"Chinese Canadian. Chinese people, we are afraid!" He clasps his hands together and pretends to shiver with fear, but he is still smiling. A lighthearted coronavirus joke and nothing more.

"Christopher," he reads. "What do you do for work?"

"I'm a doctor."

"My name is Maxwell," he announces. "I am a public health officer. One day, if I am lucky, I want to be a doctor as well. Welcome to Sierra Leone."

We emerge from the customs building in the early twilight, and the air is still, the anarchy of Parmelap behind us. The Renault 19 is waiting for us at the edge of the parking lot, once grotesque but now yellow and blue in its splendour, a sight for sore eyes. Beyond the parking lot, there are streetlights and smooth, paved highway in the direction of distant Freetown. We approach the vehicle and are unable to contain our joy. Our driver will make his delivery. The Salones are finally home. They cheer as we arrive, our mutual relief reflected on their faces as well. I still can't open the door of the car, but this time, the passengers and even the driver erupt in laughter. The ice is broken. They clap, and there are fist bumps all around. I look over at Melody and see that she is silently crying. Her face is covered with streaks of muddy tears of happiness.

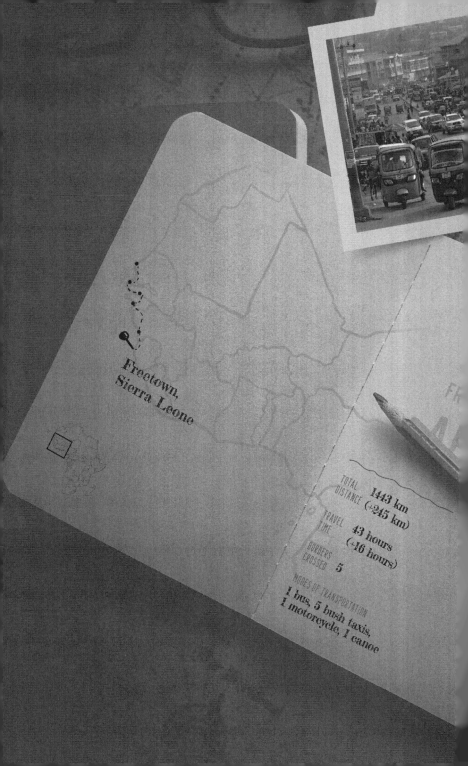

Freetown,
Sierra Leone

TOTAL **1443 km**
DISTANCE (+245 km)

TRAVEL **43 hours**
TIME (+16 hours)

BORDERS **5**
CROSSED

MODES OF TRANSPORTATION
1 bus, 5 bush taxis,
1 motorcycle, 1 canoe

Chimpanzees at the Tacugama Lodge, lobster thermidor, Afrobeats on the Lumley Beach strip, and effusively friendly locals made Sierra Leone one of our favorite stops in West Africa. This short story takes place entirely within a beach hotel in Freetown. I would describe it as a character-driven story about the unique challenges of being a foreign businessman in Africa, told from the less-than-reliable perspective of an outsider. It is a mosaic of truthful elements, arranged inside a mostly fictional frame.

THE NIGHT
WATCHMAN

"WE EXCHANGED SOME MONEY LAST NIGHT," SAYS MELODY. "We needed two wads to buy dinner. The man at the front desk told us there was a fee. But there was no fee for changing money before."

She pauses for dramatic effect, but instead, Muhamad asks the obvious question.

"Wait, wads?"

"Wads," she repeats. Melody motions with her thumb and index finger to indicate the approximate width of a stack of bills. "You know, wads of cash." In Sierra Leone, no denominations exist larger than ten thousand leones, which amounts to about one dollar. Bring an elastic band if you're planning a night on the town. Dinner will set you back two wads. Allow one more wad for late night drinks and a cab ride home, if you want to avoid a long walk in the dark. The bank machines only occasionally regurgitate cash on demand – probably on account of needing to be stuffed with thousands upon thousands of wads every morning, each of which individually is worth next to nothing.

"We just thought you should know."

Muhamad draws on his cigarette. He wears a sleeveless shirt and sandals, paired with a silver chain that hangs from his neck and a bracelet wrapped around his wrist. It's the uniform of somebody with enough authority to no longer need to wear a shirt, tie, and black jacket. His olive skin gives him away as Lebanese, like many property owners in Freetown. As he reflects on this weighty matter, his African assistant silently sweeps the floor around him.

"He has been warned before," Muhamad says finally. "This is not the first time he does something like this. We will see him in the market later, and he will exchange your money for a profit."

"Oh. It's such a small amount," I interject, feeling uncomfortably akin to a rat. "I know, it's hardly worth bothering you with it."

He stares at us again and pauses, as if more remains to be said. Then he decides to ask a question.

"Is this a vacation?"

I look at Melody, and we share a moment of mutual understanding. Most people have an image of the word vacation, and it suggests beaches, snorkelling, and an open bar, interrupted by occasional day trips. In contrast, this adventure might not be specifically categorized as *work*, but West Africa also resists being called a vacation in any traditional sense.

West Africa is best described as an *experience*. She's the blind date that you describe to your friends as somebody with personality.

"Hmmm." I stall for time. "You could say that. Maybe it's more of a road trip than a vacation."

"A cultural trip, maybe?" adds Melody.

"We're trying to explore the live music scene in West Africa, but so far, it's hard to find."

Muhamad raises his eyebrows.

"Sometimes there is live music on this street, next to the beach," he says. "But April and December is the only time for live music in Freetown. Otherwise, there are not enough people."

"Do you get many tourists here?" asks Melody.

"Never. Mostly business travelers come here. Or investors. Lebanese like me, Indian, sometimes Chinese. You are the first tourists in this hotel in four months."

IF SIERRA LEONE IS AFRICA'S SECRET BEACH DESTINATION, IT remains a secret even to the locals. Outside our hotel, Lumley Beach is deserted from top to bottom, despite being freckled with more restaurants, bars, and hotels than we can count. Hand painted signs above storefronts. Faded Ebola warnings stencilled to the cement walls flanking the main avenue.

A prominent billboard sprouts from the sidewalk next to beach:

YOU DON'T NEED TO PAY A BRIBE TO
GET YOUR CHILD IN SCHOOL.

Below it, a cartoon of a mother and daughter handing over a sizable wad of money to a balding school principal behind his desk. I can't see it from the patio where we are sitting, but I know for certain that on the opposite side, there is a similar admonition:

YOU DON'T NEED TO PAY A BRIBE TO
GET ELECTRICITY SERVICES.

Below that one, there will be a cartoon of a smiling man wearing blue overalls, carrying a toolbox and an over-sized lightbulb. Both billboard messages are aspirational, I suppose. All of this means that you definitely still do need to pay a bribe to have either of these things done, but that someone, somewhere, hopes that eventually you won't have to. In its own way, that's encouraging.

When the waiter approaches, we see that he is the same

man who shortchanged us a dollar two nights ago. He is wearing the same white shirt and black jacket as before.

"Hello again, my friends."

He approaches to drop the menus, the trace of a smile outlined on his face, and then he returns to the front desk. It's late afternoon, so he must be working here until tomorrow morning. I can't help but worry that our conversation with the hotel owner this morning may have jeopardized his livelihood.

Two boys walk up from the sand. Both are shirtless, and they stop beside the railing that separates our dining table from the beach. They could be ten years old, or fifteen.

"Mista, mista," says one of the boys, raising his hand to his lips. "Need money to buy food. We want to eat. Please suh. We have no family."

I avoid eye contact, but the boys have never known subtlety and they do not respond to it. Their gaze hangs over the table like an uncomfortable shadow.

"No," says Melody with a measure of finality, pivoting to face them directly. The boys rest motionless a few seconds longer before retreating to the beach with their shirts swinging from their wrists. One lays down in the sand and props himself up with his elbows, staring at the sky. The other wanders aimlessly in his vicinity.

The waiter returns to our table, a small pad and paper in hand. Melody has questions. She wants the cassava stew.

"Cassava stew is finished," says the waiter.

"What do you mean it's 'finished'?"

But by now, she knows exactly what he means. In West Africa, the mere presence of an item on a restaurant menu says nothing about whether it is available now or has even existed in recent memory. Stumped, Melody looks down at the menu again as the waiter stands patiently alongside.

I gaze out toward the sunset and notice a large man bearing down on the two shirtless boys across the length of the deserted beach. His strides are confident and deliberate. He is bald, with the imposing build of a soldier but not the uniform. It's incredible that I hadn't noticed him before.

"Hey!" the giant yells to them, closing the gap quickly. The boy who had been laying in the sand jumps to his feet. But they don't run from him, and given his size, neither would I.

"Is he the beach marshal?" I ask, breaking the silence.

"No. He is not anybody."

"Then what's he saying to them?"

"He is telling them exactly what I say. Go to school. Go home. If they see the beach marshal coming, they will run away. When they beg, they do not take the money to their parents. They use it on their own. They come here almost every day."

The man is waving them away from the beach, back toward the city. The boys put their shirts on and wander sluggishly in the direction of the road, their heads down. The giant continues down the beach, his work done.

"Okay," says Melody, "then I'll have the fufu."

"Fufu is not ready yet."

Melody's eyes return to the menu, so I engage with the waiter again. "What do you think of Guinea?"

"Guinea?"

"We just arrived from Guinea yesterday," I tell him. "It's much friendlier here. We like it much more in Sierra Leone."

"I like Conakry," he says. "I have friends there. Here in Freetown, there is no money. There, you work hard and there is money. But Sierra Leone is a safe place. The only problem here is that some of these kids, they like begging."

He points back towards the beach, where the same two boys have wandered back in the direction of the water, their shirts dangling from their wrists once more. They are the wasp that always finds its way back into your juice. It seems this isn't the sort of social problem that can be rectified by a single rebuke delivered by a lone good Samaritan.

The grass is always greener, I suppose.

MUHAMAD TAPS HIS CIGARETTE INTO THE ASHTRAY AND looks away, through his office window, out toward the beach, and into infinity.

"My family has been here since World War Two. I moved back here in 2013 just before Ebola. I shipped the kids back to Lebanon so they would be safe."

"And do you like it here?"

There is a pregnant pause, similar to the pause when he asked us if we were here on vacation. He meets my gaze.

"There are positives and negatives. All the infrastructure is new. Sierra Leone was developing rapidly up to 2012. The roads, many more hotels on the beach."

"And the negatives?"

He pauses again, enough time to look away through the window again, ever so briefly.

"The medical care. I hope you are healthy. Did you know there are only thirteen ventilators in this whole country? There are no specialists. Only the general practitioner." I nod. He takes a single breath, and exhales audibly. "And this hotel. This ball and chain."

"Why?"

"*They* are always after you," he says.

"Who are *they*?"

"The tax department, labour, tourism, *they*. *They* did not come today. Regulation. You have to be on top of *them* all the time. Yesterday, it was the tourism board who asked me for money."

"Well, maybe you don't have to pay," I suggest blandly.

"Ah, but *they* can blacklist the hotel. *They* can always

find some penalty. The inspectors can ask for money for any infraction."

I nod. I imagine a billboard that reads '*You don't need to pay a bribe to operate a beach hotel*' but it seems too far fetched. The corruption is endemic here. Everybody is aware of it, but it is always somebody else's problem to stamp out. The tragedy of corruption is the tragedy of the commons.

But Muhamad has not finished his cataloguing of the faults of Sierra Leone. He has forged an alliance with us, presumably because we are visibly even less African than him.

"The workers here are so lazy," he continues. "They don't care. They're just not motivated, so you can't just leave the business with someone. You have to be on top of them all the time. 'You pay too much attention to details', they say to me."

"Oh," I say again, trying to strike a tone of professional neutrality. I can't decide if his assessment is fair, culturally insensitive, or deeply racist. "But they have job security, and so many people here don't have that. Why wouldn't they work hard?"

"They think that maybe tomorrow, they'll go be a painter, or they'll go sell things on the street."

He laughs for the first time.

"I will give you an example," he says, leaning forward across the desk as if sharing a secret. "I just went to the grocery to buy some toilet paper, but I forgot my wallet. I asked my employee to go get the toilet paper. When he came back, he said they had run out. The shelf was full when I was there, *ten minutes ago*. How is it possible they have run out?"

"I suppose," I respond, "that how much effort you put into something depends on how stable you see your future."

"*CETTE RUMEUR DU CIEL AVANT QUE LA NUIT BASCULE SUR LE PORT.*"

The murmuring of the sky before darkness spills over onto the port. I recall this fragment of an evocative passage from my Albert Camus novel and scribble it hastily into my journal. Evocative because here, near the equator, the twilight is indeed short, and when night falls, it suddenly descends like a veil onto the beach. It's a beautiful sight.

The evening is transformative for the city as well. The haze over the distant hills dissolves into darkness, the weight of the oppressive heat lifts as the sunlight dissipates, and it becomes possible to move again. That liberation delivers the rising sound of music projecting across the beach from the row of restaurants and bars that line it. Nigerian Afrobeats mingle with the honking, the motorbikes, and the restless hum of the city waking up for a second time. Fruit sellers, money changers, and women in colourful dresses crowd the market streets. Every *keke* overflows with passengers as it speeds by.

There are as many disabled men on the streets of Freetown as begging children in Ziguinchor. They represent the collateral damage of the brutal eleven-year civil war that left hundreds of thousands dead and millions more internally and externally displaced. The disabled men are missing their limbs – an arm here, a leg there – and they limp about the sidewalks supported by shabby makeshift crutches. They are young, often aggressive, and sometimes surprisingly hostile.

They are also rarely alone.

In the end, I suppose none of it should be surprising.

One will approach, all smiles, an outstretched hand to greet you, but if he shakes your hand, he won't let go so easily. You will try to gently slip your hand away, but he will only squeeze it harder. Sometimes his friends will surround you, and you will continue smiling so that he will believe that you don't perceive him to be a threat. That's the lie of it, and he knows it as well as you do. And so, you with your rictus grin edge away slowly, probing any defect in their closing net – all while seeking out the reassuring bright lights of a nearby restaurant or hotel.

They rarely take no for an answer. Perhaps they *shouldn't* take no for an answer, so wretched has been their lot in life. I have little understanding of what the world owes them, if anything, and whether we ourselves are blameless. If their country took care of them, maybe they wouldn't be out here – but then again, maybe they still would. We have no way of knowing.

It's not my fault. It's not their fault. But simultaneously, somehow, both those statements are also falsehoods. Each of those men is both an individual, and simultaneously a grubby reflection of the world.

"Hello hello hello how are you money money," says an old toothless woman clad in a blue hijab. We shake our heads and continue walking. When we arrive at the gates of our hotel, the night watchman is waiting for us, clad in his customary white shirt and black jacket. He unlocks the gate.

"You are welcome," he says as we enter.

"BRING THE WOMEN IN AT TEN O'CLOCK," SAYS A DISTIN-guished white woman. Her British accent is refined. She is typing on her laptop with one hand, holding her smartphone with the other. "We want them to tell their story, all of that business."

There's something vaguely unsettling about her statement, just as there's something unsettling about this tasteful and well-appointed breakfast sanctuary. I can't describe the feeling precisely. It is as if parading impoverished Sierra Leonean women *in* at a specified hour to commoditize their story for appraisal by white benefactors must be something obscene. But it might also be exactly what is appropriate. As usual, I have no way to know.

Melody makes her way downstairs to join me in the hotel lounge a short time later, her disproportionately large single backpack giving her the unfortunate appearance of a pack mule. She's brought with her an array of sausages, crêpes, and flaky pastries from the buffet, and I help myself to another Danish from her plate. It's still warm. Beyond the reception desk, I see Muhamad descend the stairs, and when he notices us, he detours to stop by our table. He greets the British woman with a polite nod and a short wave, and then turns to us.

"We're leaving today for Tiwai Island," I tell him. "And then Liberia after that."

"Very nice and thank you for staying here. Come to my office please, to say goodbye before you leave," says Muhamad. We don't tell him that we've filled the crevices of our backpacks with stolen croissants and buns from the ample buffet, which we will eat on our way to Tiwai. I'm sure we're not the first to sneak food away from a breakfast buffet.

When we've finished, we make our way to Muhamad's office. He shuts the door behind us and beckons us to sit down. Then he sits as well and leans forward over his desk, his hands tightly clasped over a pile of documents.

"I released him from his job this morning. The night watchman. I have to do what is best for my business."

I nod. I'm not sure yet how I feel about that.

"I don't think it's right for him to take advantage of tourists like that," says Melody.

"I think that makes sense," I say slowly, as if I have the slightest clue how to own and operate a hotel in Sierra Leone. "If he does it and you catch him, it probably means it isn't the first time nor the last time."

On the other hand, we're dealing with less than a dollar. That decision to risk one's livelihood for such a meagre amount is almost as unfathomable as the decision to fire someone for it.

"It is for the best," Muhamad insists. "He will find something else to do, maybe. Maybe he changes money on the street, in the market."

"It will be a bit of a pay cut, I would imagine," I say, not quite sure how to respond.

"I have been here many years," he continues, "but we are not the same. I am Lebanese, and I have my business. *They* will not feel sorry for me if my business fails. *They* will never accept me here as African. So I do what I feel I have to do."

He allows his words to hang aerosolized between us. The room is silent, save for the muffled clattering of plates behind the closed door.

"Let me tell you another story, and then I will let you leave. Once, I encountered several young men, who had some drinks. They saw me and they approached me."

Muhamad folds his hands together in front of his mouth and looks away, reflective.

"They grabbed me by the scruff of the neck."

"Why?" I ask.

"Why does anyone do anything? They were men, and they were drunk."

"Sometimes that's enough."

He nods, and then continues.

"There is an old saying that my English is not good enough to properly say. They told me that if you throw the wood in the water, it will turn dark. But even if the wood change colour, it will always try to get back to the same colour. The Lebanese, we are the wood. We will never be African."

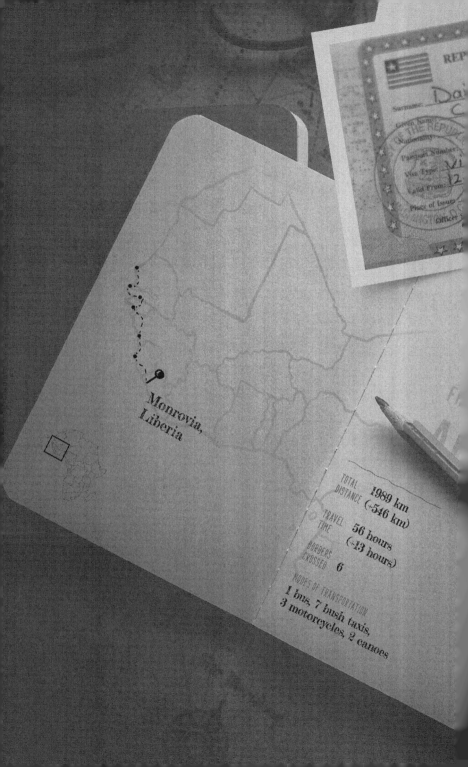

War-torn Liberia was founded by emancipated slaves from the United States, and as such, it exists at times as a bizarre and dystopian rendition of its parent. This is another character-driven story, one about the determined and resourceful caretaker of the famous Ducor Hotel in Monrovia, and my limited role as an observer and witness. This is a story that could not have happened without the aid of a surreptitious recording device, such are the nearly incomprehensible accents of Liberian English.

CARETAKER
ON THE HILL

THERE IS GARBAGE EVERYWHERE IN DOWNTOWN MON-
rovia. Down below the bridge – next to the slums – the
water is choked with it. If you look closely, you can make
out the plastic bags, Styrofoam cups, discarded shoes, used
diapers, and tattered cardboard. The objects float lazily in
the cove as tiny islands of waste, before finally washing
up on the shore in colourful heaps. Once moored, they
become as much a permanent feature of the beach as the
shantytown beside it.

The shantytown itself is like many, and I suppose one
image of poverty blurs easily into the next. But there,
painted on one of the walls of a shack on the beach, there
is a flag. Red, white, and blue. Star and stripes. Blink twice,
and it could be America.

Up above, near the bridge where we consult our map, three children play football on the street. In America, they would call it soccer, but that's a long way from Liberia. They have plenty of room to run, because the traffic is scant here at least.

But when we turn a corner, we see that a lengthy queue has formed at the gas station, in large part because there is still no gasoline. If you insist on gasoline but can't wait, it's best to visit one of the fuel speakeasies. They're not hard to find. They sell gasoline in glass wine bottles beside the road, but it won't come cheap.

"There's a good one," says Melody as we walk. She points out a mural on a concrete wall. The mural declares:

THERE IS NO HONOR IN HONOR KILLING

It hadn't specifically occurred to me before, but now faced with these words, I decide that I already agree with this sentiment. Monrovia is filled with lovingly painted murals designed to engineer behaviours that should be obvious. Maybe they are obvious to most people. I can only hope.

"Where you goin'?" asks a woman with loud hair. There's a curious American lilt to her speech. In Detroit, they would call it sass, but that's a long way from Monrovia. She's sitting next to her greasy spoon restaurant with a toothpick emerging from her mouth.

"The Ducor Hotel," I say. "Are we going the right way?"

"Yeah," she says. "But yawl be careful. Liberia is not so safe." Because she wants us to keep safe.

We continue onward, towards the market. Police officers wearing second hand American-issue uniforms roam the city centre. So too do the ubiquitous yellow *kekes*. A *keke* is identical to what would be known as a *tuk-tuk* in Thailand, a lightweight three-wheeled vehicle with a fabric roof. Somewhere, someone told me they were called that because of the *tuk-tuk* sound the motor makes as it putters down the street. The *keke* makes a similar sound, come to think of it.

Once we are within the congested streets of the Waterside market, however, the *kekes* can no longer pass through. There's just no room. Instead, there are four rows of vendors spilling onto each side of the street, one pressed up against the next. I've never seen anything like it. With some luck, and clinging desperately to our pockets, we manage to squeeze through the gaps in the crowd, somehow without trampling on the blankets covered in produce, shoes, and other assorted merchandise in the process. When we clear the market, there is another mural painted on another concrete wall.

This time, the mural reads:

A WOMAN IS YOUR FRIEND.
DO NOT BEAT ON HER.
LOVE, CHERISH, AND PROTECT HER.

With one hand, the man painted on the mural has removed his belt and raised it over his head. His teeth are clenched, and with his other hand, he is clutching a woman's blouse as she attempts to crawl away on her knees. Beneath his legs, a crying infant in a diaper looks up at his father.

"I am fully on board with this message," I say.

"It's a little on the nose, I admit," says Melody.

We again discreetly check the map, then climb the hill that leads away from the market. Here, the paved road suddenly ends and becomes a well-marked dirt trail. Children play football under the canopy of the trees, chasing each other back and forth among still more piles of trash.

At the top of the trail, a grand stone statue of a man stands sentry, shaded by the foliage and perched atop an enormous pedestal that is nearly my height. A paved parking lot surrounds it, along with a food stand, a purple umbrella, and two figures reclining in plastic chairs. An old man, and a young man.

"You want a tour of the statue and history Liberia, you let me know," the old man shouts at us from his seat. "I been here sixteen good years."

We pass them by. Beyond them lies a chain link fence and a gate – and beyond that, the crumbling ruins of the abandoned Ducor Hotel.

THE GUARD MAKES US WAIT BEHIND THE GATE WITHOUT explanation. He is uniformed, but his brown pants are faded and badly torn at the pocket. Behind us, a wedding party has arrived in the parking lot for their photo shoot. The bride wears a white dress, the groom a bright orange tuxedo, and a photographer carries a large professional camera that looks identical to mine. The summit is not a beautiful place – there's too much garbage, too much broken asphalt – and yet they take pictures anyway.

"Wussup man."

The same young man approaches from his food stand, and for a small bribe, the guard allows us to pass. We walk towards the ruins of the hotel, which form eight stories of stark grey concrete.

"Do you get many tourists here?" I ask him.

"Two, three, one every day," he says. It's a vaguely American twang, a Southern drawl mixed with an African accent. He tells us his name is James, and he walks a few comfortable steps ahead, leading us inside.

"Ducor built in 1970," James begins. "In the eighties, war. Nineties, war. Destroy. Everything looted. People live in here. They threw them out."

"This is where they keep the water." He points to a column in the middle of the ruins of what may have once been the lobby. "Ten million gallons for the entire hotel."

Melody knows all this already. She's been reading about it, and therefore by extension, I've been hearing about it. The five-star hotel was shut in 1989 just before the brutal civil war in Liberia, in which Charles Taylor's army battled Prince Johnson's rebels for control of Monrovia. Over a thousand refugees camped in the ruins of the Ducor beginning in 2003, until they were finally evicted in 2007. Since then, visitors have tried to recreate the faded grandeur of the historic site.

"Sometimes rappers come make music videos. Tourist make photoshoots in the bathtubs. Picnic. Yoga session. Wedding. One Scotsman bring his bagpipes. He piping through every country in the world, kilt and all."

"Interesting."

"Qaddafi was going to restore it, but they killed him," says James.

"Who owns it now?"

"Private entity. The boss."

Grass and shrubs sprout through the cracked remains of the floor tiles. An enormous cobweb hangs from the wall of what was once the conference hall. A short walk from there, we find a dancefloor whose walls are decorated with beautiful murals. James tells us that after the wars, people squatted here too.

"Do they still hold dances here?" I ask.

"No. Boss wouldn't allow it."

We climb the concrete stairwell, floor by floor, until there is nowhere left to climb. From the roof of the hotel, we can see Westpoint, the downtown ghetto, with its endless rows of tin roofs, save for the buildings that have no roofs at all. Palm trees speckle the shoreline. Here at the summit of this ruined luxury hotel, the trash that clogs the beach isn't nearly as visible. And on the other side of the rooftop, a seemingly endless Atlantic vista unfolds into the horizon.

Behind the hotel, there is an enormous cotton tree, nearly as large as the entire hotel itself. It abuts the American embassy compound, which represents the grandest building in the Monrovia cityscape. The cotton tree shades both the children below, who are still playing football, and the statue on its pedestal. It is also filled with hundreds of bats, whose silhouettes hang from the branches like bunches of fruit.

"What's with all the bats?" I ask James.

"Cotton tree important to them. America keep the bats. America don't want people looking into the embassy."

BY THE TIME WE EMERGE FROM THE HOTEL, THE SUN HAS washed all the subtlety out of the sky, burning it the uniformly blinding white of freshly laundered bedsheets. We pay James for his time and follow him again as he traces his way back towards the purple umbrella. The old man remains there in its modest shade, sprawled on his plastic chair. Melody wanders away towards the statue, but I pause next to this old man. He's every bit as much a part of Liberia as this broken hotel. I'd like to talk to him, but I'm not quite sure what to say, nor does he even acknowledge my presence.

His two canes lean up against a plastic table. He wears a tattered blue shirt and shorts. His left leg has been eaten away by disease, a grotesque indentation that no one has bothered to bandage, and which stretches haphazardly from his ankle to his knee. A Buruli ulcer, I assume.

"Does it hurt?" I ask, feeling foolish as soon as the question has left my mouth.

"Yeah, it hurt."

At first, he ignores me and talks only to James, who has posted himself in the second plastic chair beside the store. But when I ask about the tour, the old man leaps up with surprising agility, deftly takes command of his two canes and races towards the steps of the statue. James jumps up as well, easily outpaces the old man, and beckons for me to follow him. But I don't want James. I want the old man with the canes. And the old man, it seems, suddenly wants me.

"I don't need you here," he shouts to James as he catapults his way up the steps with acrobatic agility, disappearing into the enveloping shade of the cotton tree. I follow him, attempting to match his pace. The old man is distracted, however, when he encounters four more visitors pacing languidly around the base of the statue.

"You need pay me," he immediately demands as he rounds the corner. This demand is directed not at me, but towards a stout bald man who is inspecting the carvings on the pedestal with his family, presumably his wife and two children. The bald man has impeccable posture despite his unapologetic potbelly, and he wears an elegant lavender dashiki.

"You cannot charge people," the bald man scolds him without hesitation. "You let people give of their own volition."

The old man shrinks away slightly, then regains his composure. He is the unstoppable force who has finally collided with an immoveable object. But he knows when he is defeated, and so he announces that the tour will begin in earnest.

He poses on his two canes, and begins his discourse with an appeal to high drama, raising his voice so that it can be heard above the din of distant motors and shouts of children:

"Liberia founded by slaves from the Great United States of America."

This, too, would be something that Melody knew already. That abolitionists, unhappy with racial discrimination in the United States, took to the ocean with emancipated slaves as settlers to West Africa. They imagined a new American state, in its idealized first incarnation, founded upon the same high and noble principles – and later, built a looking-glass vision of that same union. Its first president, immortalized above us now in faded bronze, was a mixed-race man born free in Virginia who emigrated to Liberia under the auspices of the American Colonization Society.

But having escaped oppression and servitude in the United States, the freed slaves carried on the legacy of their oppressors. The indigenous in Africa emerged as an underclass in the newly formed Liberian state, the lowest rung in a new cultural and racial caste system that placed Americo-Liberians at the top and indigenous blacks at the bottom. The irony is simultaneously tragic and poetic.

We circumnavigate the square base of the statue, inch by inch, and with each successive relief that is carved into the stone, the caretaker explains its origins and meaning. The heroic journey of the Americo-Liberians from their humble beginnings in chains and servitude, to their settlements on the coast of Africa, to the triumph of freedom and independence. But it is a path which ultimately led to a present-day state that resembles the Great United States of America only in the most dystopian of ways.

"After the 1990 war," continues the caretaker, "this place was totally abandoned by the confused government and the Liberian people. So, I'm the one who told them: do not toilet here, do not gamble here anymore."

"This man grandfather was the caretaker of the hotel when he was a little baby. And he saw me working. I told them clean up this swimming pool. I said no more fire brandy. Nobody play gamble here."

I think he means that he took responsibility for managing the property surrounding the hotel, clearing out those who would let this historic site fall into ruin. But his accent makes it difficult for me to follow his discourse, and Melody has since faded into the background, having given up on the struggle to decode his diction. The bald man seems to have no such difficulty. He is listening intently, hanging on the caretaker's every word.

THE CARETAKER STOPS SPEAKING AND EXAMINES EACH member of his modest congregation. James looks on from a comfortable distance, as do several teenagers who have stopped playing football to join us on the pedestal. The bald man rests his hands on the shoulders of his two children. Then he nods pensively and strokes his chin.

"Are you being taken care of by the Minister of Information?" asks the bald man.

The caretaker sits down at the base of the statue, in

the shadow of the first president, and leans both his canes against the stone. From here, his left leg looks awful. The ulcer is bumpy, irregular, and profound. Its centre is flaming crimson outlined by a ridge of purulent yellow. It will never heal without extensive surgical grafting.

"I went to the Ministry to tell them I was going to manage this," says the caretaker. "But they see me in this condition. The past president come here and give me small money. So, I'm here sixteen good years. Government don't give me any money."

"It's a compelling story," replies the bald man, now looming over him from above. "You should be taken care of by the Ministry of Information, the Ministry of Culture or Tourism. Even if this place owned by the Methodists, it's a government site, a tourist site."

I don't understand what Methodists have to do with a statue of the first president of Liberia, so I quietly ask the bald man for some clarity. He is an intimidating presence, and I am somewhat reluctant to interrupt him with my ignorance.

"There's a large portion of land owned by the settlers. This site is claimed by the Methodists. Any time it's a private property, you don't go on it for anything. Maybe that's where the government is coming from. But *be that as it may*, it is a tourist site, so the government has some part to play in maintaining it, providing *security* for this monument."

He looks over at me. I'm listening intently but struggling to keep up with his thick Liberian accent. By the time his sentences end, I'm still three words behind.

"Your phone could be snatched off and that can be scary," he says, pointing to my Samsung and then turning back to the caretaker. "Most of these are foreigners, and they go back and they say Liberia is not safe."

"But the president is a man who is development oriented. He is a man who has the country at heart. I can assure you. The minute he comes here, your story will change. He is an open person."

I wonder if this bald man is political, if he is in the current president's pocket. Whatever the case may be, his presence is commanding, and the caretaker is now fully engaged in his discourse. He leans forward, listening eagerly.

"See how I am? See ma' teeth?" The caretaker flashes an incomplete row of rotted teeth. "I hardly get food to eat. I told them, gentlemen, no! You can't be like that!"

"Time will come, you will be surprised," answers the bald man. "The minute he visit here. He has a passion. He has a plan. But the Methodists will try to discourage the government. They will try to claim the place. They will say they got the property."

"You got *big money*," says the bald man scornfully, gesticulating, and for a brief moment it's not clear that he's still referring to the Methodists. "But you gotta be able to maintain the place. And then the place become a tourist site, you're gonna make money fo' your church!"

"…but it don't have no security, nobody to guard it, fo' the entire place, the entire hill…"

"You ever have any journalist come here? They put you on the television?"

"Yeah!" exclaims the caretaker. "Journalist come here!"

I can't discern if he means that journalists have been here before, or that he would welcome them to come in the future. But the implication is clear. That perhaps if his situation were more public, his luck would change. That he might be one televised human-interest story away from the arrival of a wealthy benefactor to look after his health and welfare. Nevertheless, the bald man has another concern.

"You see, the Liberian, we don' like each otha'."

The chorus of gathered Liberians nod in agreement. "Exactly," one murmurs in the background.

James breaks into the conversation: "You try go to the office fo' help, and you can' ever get it. When people come here, they give him a dolla', two dolla', it doesn't solve the problem. He had to go to hospital, no money."

"Actually, life is unfair," says the bald man. "Every guy is responsible for his own destiny. And there is no way to change that. I'm a director, not a lawmaker."

"God can lift you up, you understand," he continues. "If you have a kind heart, you know? As a result, God begin to bless you. So what you doin' here is *completing your quota* for this country. And it will not go unnoticed. If it does not come to you directly, it will come to your offspring. And history will say, this guy did some sacrificial stuff. Even if we human beings cannot recognize now that you have a kind heart."

"Thank you, God bless."

"I pay school fees. I pay rent. But somebody connected to you, either your child, someone in the bloodline, will benefit *immensely* because his father or his uncle made a contribution to the development. History will say, there was a guy who used to do some helpful things."

"Thank you, God bless."

"I will try for you, I can't make a promise. I can't give you money. Maybe you're expecting money. The cripple (if you're a believer) was expecting Peter to give him money, but Peter tol' him, he said, I don't have any money. So don't give up."

I don't specifically remember this passage from the Bible, but I take it on faith that he is accurately paraphrasing the Good Book. I am surprised that there is no money attached to his kind words. No promises attached to his generous blessings. But if the caretaker is disappointed, he doesn't make it evident.

"So thank you so much for being so patriotic," the bald man continues. "I didn't know this situation was happening. I'm moved. Methodist have every reason to identify with you. But they prefer to go out into the street, give people food, take photos. I feel very, very discouraged. But now I am encouraged. You provide education. It's historical."

"Thank you," the caretaker says once more.

"You are blessed now, brother."

There is a pregnant pause while the bald man reaches into his dashiki and produces a business card. He leans forward and hands it to the caretaker, who accepts it with both hands. He continues looking at it, even after the bald man and his wife have collected their two children and led them by their shoulders back down the steps of the monument, out from under the shadows of the looming cotton tree, retreating back down the dirt trail and toward the noise, the traffic, and the congestion of Monrovia.

Man, Côte
D'Ivoire

TOTAL
DISTANCE 2458 km
          (-469 km)

TRAVEL
TIME   67 hours
        (-11 hours)

BORDERS
CROSSED 7

MODES OF TRANSPORTATION
2 buses, 2 bush taxis,
5 motorcycles, 2 canoes

Considering that the journey from Monrovia to the border town of Man involved a bush taxi and two motorcycles (the driver of the first who *may* have been intoxicated, and second of whom punctured his tire at sunset in the middle of the jungle), I'm still not sure why this is the particular story I chose for Côte D'Ivoire. Nonetheless, the enigmatic title refers to a genre of Ivorian popular dance music. It wasn't until I learned more about the origins of the name that it struck me as an apt title for this tale. *Coupé décalé* is an insignificant short story about the tension between our timidly Canadian moral centres and the shamelessness of a traveling huckster aboard an intercity bus.

COUPÉ DÉCALÉ

Coupé: *faire un coup*; steal or deceive (in Nouchi, an Ivorian slang)

Décalé: disappear or run away

1. Going abroad to unscrupulously make gains and return home to *travailler* (party and distribute cash)
2. Akoupé ethnicity of Côte D'Ivoire: a dance executed with cutlasses
3. A dance choreography consisting of diagonally slicing the air with the edge of the hand (*coupé*)
4. None of the above
5. All of the above

THE LEAP FROM THE TEMPERATE IVORIAN MOUNTAIN TOWN of Man to the lowland capital of Yamoussoukro should take about six hours, or at least that's what the Dutch traveller told us yesterday. He promised us a large, modern bus, a sealed highway, air conditioning, and plenty of leg room. At a glance, the bus station in central Man even superficially resembles a modern bus station, with its standard ticket window and orderly waiting room furnished with rows of permanent plastic chairs.

But the day is off to a slow start. It's an hour past departure time, and the platform is still empty. Maybe our bus will arrive soon. Maybe it will arrive never. West Africa quickly teaches you to live in the present.

That same Dutch traveler told us to make sure that the bus company was named *UTB*. Then again, that same Dutch traveler also claimed, when asked, that his favorite two countries in the entire world were Tchad and Somaliland. He explained that he derived an almost euphoric pleasure from ten hours of continuous hiking in the equatorial sun. On the whole, I found him to be a tall, arrogant contrarian, and so I deliberately ignored his bus recommendations. Any bus that this Dutch traveler would choose was not the bus for me.

When our bus finally does rumble through the iron gates of the station, it has presumably arrived from another more distant location because it is already packed with passengers. Every window seat is occupied, as well as most of the middle and aisle seats.

There is no air conditioning. Resigned to the predicament, most of the passengers have already opened their windows. Others simply fan their damp faces with folded newspapers.

But there is something else visibly wrong with this bus. It's too small. It has clearly been refurbished to squeeze even more passengers inside. I can't decide exactly how they've managed this – whether the seats themselves are smaller, or if they have simply been pushed closer together – but the end result is that there are three seats on one side of the aisle, and two on the other. The central aisle itself has been all but obliterated, leaving just enough room for an average sized passenger to squeeze his way through lengthwise while crushing stray arms and errant feet along his path.

We choose the middle and aisle seats of a three-seater. I take the aisle, and when I stretch my legs, I step on the sandaled foot of the man beside me. Next to the window, a wrinkled old woman wearing a black veil is folded up like an ironing board. She's vanishingly tiny, but still somehow manages to crowd Melody's space.

It's rare that the central characteristic of a place is the heat. But in Côte D'Ivoire, grumbling over the heat is more than mere small talk. The temperature is uniform, in all places, at all times, even here in the mountains. To ignore that heat would be to disingenuously ignore the first thing on one's mind, all the time. It's worse inside, whether it's poorly ventilated concrete buildings or the inside of this stationary bus, where the air flow is stagnant and oppressive.

Thirty degrees, but it feels like thirty-seven with the humidity. Each body movement is slow, precise, and deliberate, a sloth-like calculation before committing to the slightest expenditure of energy. Then there's the humidity, the stubborn sweat that just will not evaporate. Everyone is covered in sweat, all the time. The only remedy is the small white dishtowel that locals carry to mop the perspiration from their brows when they stop to rest.

We are coated in the filth, dirt, and dust that adhere to that sweat. Melody's eyelash extensions may never be the same. Their individual hairs are clumped and tinged an unfortunate cinnamon colour, although I would never tell her so. It would only invite ridicule, because my own hair is no better. When I run my fingers through it, it feels as though it has been powdered. Another month here and I would be dreadlocked.

THE ROAD TO YAMOUSSOUKRO IS SURPRISINGLY ROUGH. It is a single lane, narrow and potholed, upon which the bus crawls towards the capital city in fits and starts. At times, the fits last longer than the starts.

Two hours into the journey, a man three rows in front of us climbs to his feet, shifting his body to face the rear of the bus. He's clad in a button up shirt, the sleeves rolled up to his elbows. His shirt is clean and meticulously patterned, embroidered with a dizzying pattern of overlapping red, white, and blue circles. Stubble, but the sort that is scrupulously groomed, and which frames a square chin and intense eyes. I hadn't noticed him before, which must mean that he boarded the bus somewhere along our route. He is not the type of man whose presence would be easily overlooked.

He rests his hands on the seats beside him to maintain his balance as the bus ricochets back and forth on the uneven road. As he does so, his eyes explore the shoulder to shoulder cramped passengers, as if he is scouring the scene for something or someone. For several seconds he says nothing at all. His eyes rest briefly on me, and then noticeably longer on Melody. I suppose the eye is drawn to the unique, and an Asian female on an intercity bus in West Africa certainly qualifies as that.

"I come from Burkina Faso, but now I live in Côte D'Ivoire," he announces in French, before allowing a pregnant silence to hang in the air. His voice is powerful and resonant, his expression severe. I turn my head to gauge the reaction of the other passengers. Some have looked up, startled, while others continue sleeping.

"And I come to you with words of wisdom and truth," the man continues, "which will change your life for the better."

I look over at Melody because I anticipate where this is going. With a modicum of luck, his pitch will be brief, after which we can sink again into the lethargic half-slumber that accounts for the bulk of these long bus journeys. But not with this man. Public speaking and showmanship flow through his veins. The seconds blur into minutes, and the minutes become an hour of unbroken monologue. He is a consummate professional – from the rise and fall of his pitch, to its varying cadence, the flow of his words punctuated by short staccato bursts, to the calculated pauses that hang in the air to allow rare moments of reflection.

And still he continues. Over the monotonous hum of the engine, I can't fully understand everything he is saying in French, but he's equally impossible to simply ignore. He has the voice and commanding presence of a Southern Baptist preacher. I insert my earbuds, turn up the music, but it is to no avail. I register that he is preaching something about God – something about religion, perhaps Christianity but more likely Islam. My brain unwillingly tracks his every transition, now from the ravages of diabetes, to the devastation of strokes, to the hallmarks of vascular disease, and finally to the classic signs of Bell's palsy.

It's much too hot inside the bus to listen to him.

"I wish he would shut up," I say to Melody.

"Is he even allowed to do this? Can we tell him to shut up?" Melody says.

I'm not sure. Without missing a beat, he seems to have moved on to erectile dysfunction. He thrusts a brief masturbatory gesture toward his audience that requires no particular French-English interpretation. We both laugh at the shamelessness of it all.

I look back over my shoulder at the remainder of the bus. The man behind me is crouched forward in repose, and my elbow bangs against his head when I move. About two thirds of the passengers are sleeping, against formidable odds, or at least pretending to do so. But another third of the bus seems mesmerized by this man's resonant, booming voice. A young woman behind me catches my eye. She wears a mischievous grin that suggests she understands more English than she lets on.

When I turn my head back, there is a lengthy pause in his monologue, and although I am looking down, I can feel the weight of his gaze on my forehead. It forces me to look up, and sure enough, he is staring directly at me, expressionless. I remove my earbuds and stare back, challenging him to break his gaze. Suddenly, we are two predators in the wild, sizing each other up.

Then he leans forward and whispers to me in English:

"You no speak French."

"*Seulement un peu,*" I say.

He moistens his lips. "Come and see my snake. I have a snake in my bag."

I force a strained laugh. I don't know if this is a sexual euphemism, a statement of fact, or something botched in translation. "Excuse me?"

"Come and see my snake."

"I don't think I understand." If his goal is to confuse me, he has succeeded. Melody shrugs. I look back at the young woman behind me for help, and although she appears thoroughly engaged in our interaction, she offers no insights. And with that, the man draws himself up again to his full height and resumes his monologue.

THE BUS COMES TO A STOP IN A SMALL TOWN, AND WHAT little air circulation we had previously been afforded immediately congeals. Many of the passengers haphazardly disembark, shuffling away in various directions to stretch their legs, purchase food and drink from the vendors gathered beside the road, or toilet in the scorched brush beyond. The vendors have anticipated our arrival, because they crowd the front and back doors of the bus, displaying their baskets of merchandise against the windows, jockeying for our attention. Some of them are children, with battle-weary faces that suggest they might be eight years old, going on eighty. We remain in our cramped seats, since leaving the bus is a sure-fire recipe for being abandoned in the Ivorian countryside.

The man edges forward, towards our seats, and I can feel the intensity of his eyes resting on me. This time, I'm looking away from him, out the window, but like conscience or guilt, the weight of a gaze can be inexplicably heavy.

"Hello," he says in English.

"Hello," I reply, my token attempt to smile reduced to a brief and forced spasm of the cheeks. It's insufferably hot and I am unwilling to disguise my growing annoyance with him and the endless monologue to which he has subjected us.

"You no speak French."

"No," I say this time.

"I speak English small-small."

"That's good."

"Where are you from?"

"Canada."

"Give me your Facebook, What's App. I want to come to Canada." His eyes dart between Melody and I, as if he can't decide which of us is the better mark.

"Uh, my phone doesn't work here," I say, slurring my words together in the hopes of confounding him. Maybe then he will stop staring. "I don't have the right SIM card."

"Why do you want my Facebook?" demands Melody. "I only give my Facebook to my friends, and we are not friends."

It comes out with a bluntness that makes me uncomfortable, but maybe a little bluntness is just what the doctor ordered.

"I don't understand when you talk fast-fast," he says, holding my gaze for several seconds more before losing interest and looking away.

The driver honks. The passengers slowly begin to file back into the bus, some in possession of white plastic bags filled with assorted sundries. The vendors make their final pleas, waving and tapping with desperation at the windows. We pull back out onto the highway.

The woman behind taps me on the shoulder, and Melody turns as well.

"You are not from here," says the smiling woman, and nods toward the man standing above us. He is oblivious to our conversation. "I apologize for this."

"Is he…allowed to disturb everybody on the bus like this?" asks Melody.

"They buy a place on the bus. They make an agreement with the bus company."

"Ah, so you're saying he's like a traveling YouTube ad," I say. "He's part of the price of riding the bus."

"Yes, exactly," she says, smiling. "I apologize for this."

"Does he at least…pay more for them to let him talk?"

"No, the prices are still the same. He has a ticket, like everybody else."

"And people here are okay with that? With him shouting at us all the way to Yamoussoukro?"

She shrugs, ambivalent. "He is like everyone. He need to eat, he need to put his kids in school."

HE IS EMPHATICALLY SHOUTING NOW. WE CAN'T DROWN him out.

We've tried. In a petty attempt to answer obnoxiousness with obnoxiousness, Melody and I discuss tomorrow's plans for Yamoussoukro, but make no attempt to lower our voices. We're entitled to that. Or at least, we're no less entitled than this man is entitled to deliver his endless, unsolicited sermon. For my part, I concentrate on the fundamentals of maintaining an upright posture. Deep breathing from the diaphragm. All directed to the goal of ensuring that my voice resonates through the entirety of the bus as much as possible.

If this man notices, it doesn't show. The modest power of my voice is eclipsed by an order of magnitude. If anything, his confidence and enthusiasm are growing, and with them the decibel level with which his voice booms across the bus.

By now, he has transitioned into peddling what appears to be a panacea, a miracle cure. There was a method to his madness after all, in intention behind his inventory of the many unpleasant ailments that could befall us. It is this, his prestige, his medical miracle which he would be willing to share with us for a mere five hundred francs per package. Mix two tablets in the morning, he tells us. Take it at night with water. There's no other explication, save for a white sticker affixed to the tiny transparent bag which reads *Mystère Indien*. A mystery indeed.

Raise your hand if you would like this mystery to be yours.

I turn again to look over my shoulder at the passengers behind me. I expect him to be shouted down. I expect him to be roughly escorted off the bus by an angry mob. Instead, nearly half the bus is captivated, held to rapt attention. Some are asleep, to be sure, but at least half the passengers have their hands in the air, patiently waiting for their chance to partake in the mystery. The salesman slowly makes his way down the aisle, distributing Ziploc baggies and bouncing to and fro against the seats as the bus rocks back and forth on the highway.

"What do you think is in it?" asks Melody.

"I have no idea. Some sort of detoxifying traditional medicine, I think. Or rat poison, who knows."

"Excuse me," says Melody, leaning across my body to catch the attention of the man opposite. "Can I take a look at your medicine, please?"

He surrenders his transparent plastic baggie, which contains six small, circular tablets. I look closer. Each tablet is marked with the letters 'VC'. I enter its size, shape, and markings into the pill recognition app on my phone. Nothing. As far as the pharmaceutical world is concerned, this medicine doesn't exist.

I hand the baggie back to its owner and count the number of passengers who are holding a similar purchase. Twenty-six.

"Traditional medicine," offers the woman behind me, leaning forward. "First, maybe people try this, and if it doesn't work, they go to the hospital. Or maybe they go to the hospital first, and if it doesn't work, they use traditional medicine."

"But this medicine doesn't work," I say to her, "and I think he knows that."

That realization suddenly makes me angry. What he is selling here is magic beans. The people aboard this bus don't have much, but what little they have, they are willingly surrendering to this traveling peddler in the hopes that he's stumbled upon a magical elixir. Maybe hope is enough. After all, a placebo won't work if you understand the con. Maybe they are paying for his virtuoso performance, a tip for the busker. Or perhaps he is just another soap box salesman like any other, a traveling televangelist with a bag of snake oil and empty promises.

The bus is slowing down as we approach a town centre. Outside, the street hawkers know exactly where the bus will stumble over the potholes, and they chase behind waving their merchandise as we pass. The bus briefly stops entirely, and as we begin to accelerate again, I see that it was to allow a disabled man to cross the road in front of us. The man has strapped two blackboard erasers to his hands, and he uses them to lift his body and drag his legs along behind him.

"Excuse me!" I shout to the salesman, who looms above me again. I've decided to be incensed, but I don't have much time. "What is in the medicine in the bags?"

"Sir?" adds Melody. "What are the ingredients?"

"Excuse me?" I repeat, but the salesman is already counting his money.

"He is not interested in you anymore," says the woman behind. "He already got what he wants."

The bus comes to a stop and the doors open. Blinding sunlight streams into the bus. We're too late, if there had ever been any hope, if there even should have been a hope for two foreigners on a bus traveling through Côte D'Ivoire. And with that, the medicine man retrieves his satchel from his seat and departs the bus in a flash of red, white, and blue that evaporates into the crowd of merchants below.

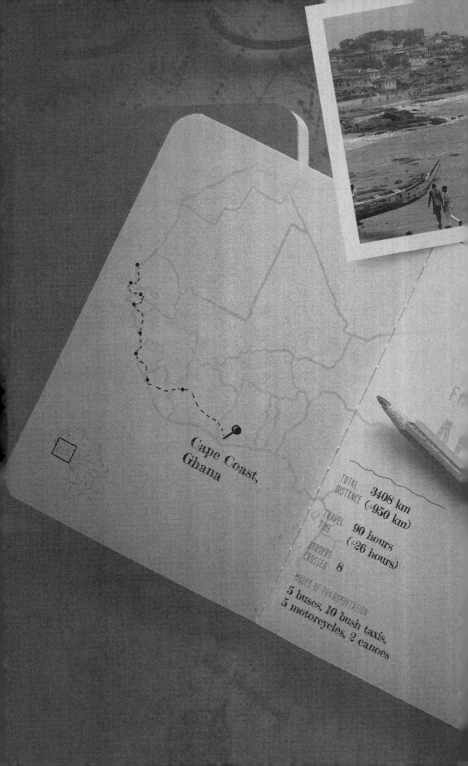

Cape Coast,
Ghana

TOTAL
DISTANCE

3408 km
(÷950 km)

TRAVEL
TIME

90 hours
(÷26 hours)

BORDERS
CROSSED

8

MODES OF TRANSPORTATION

5 buses, 10 bush taxis,
5 motorcycles, 2 canoes

Like it or not, Ghana is synonymous with slavery. This short story is a composite of a series of challenging conversations I had in Cape Coast and Accra surrounding the old trope of *finding one's roots*, and my own attempts to make sense of its contradictions. First, I'm reminded of the ancient cliché that *those who forget history are doomed to repeat it* – which invites the paradox that those who live in the past have no present or future. Second, as a person of mixed ethnicity, I am uniquely aware of the contradictions of treating people as part of identity collective, rather than simply as individuals who are absolved of the sins of their fathers. This story was the most difficult. While many of its elements are simply recorded history – that didn't make them any less worthy of being written again.

VICTIM

WHEN THE CONTINENTAL EUROPEANS APPEARED ON THE Gold Coast of Africa five hundred years ago, they stole many things, but one thing they left them with was a new religion.

The early hints of this are revealed in the billboards flanking the avenues of Cape Coast, most of which advertise either evangelical churches or approaching religious celebrations. But the Coca-Cola sign on the wall of the *Thank You Jesus* restaurant is more immediate proof of their devotion.

That sign reads:

OPEN HAPPINESS

Which would be innocuous enough, except that beside that dated corporate slogan, somebody has added in black permanent marker:

(BY THE GRACE OF GOD)

The British colonized Ghana too, whether through conquest or purchase. I suppose they would have preferred to leave the natives with the full richness of their English language. But in most cases, this didn't work out nearly as well as they might have liked. While it's true that nearly all the signs and billboards in Ghana are written in English, you won't usually hear locals speak it unless they are in an elementary school classroom, forced, or sometimes both.

And perhaps because a rarely used language fails to evolve, most written materials here make use of an oddly formal type of British English – as if the place has been frozen in amber for centuries. For example, one job advertisement calls for *obedient employees*, a phrasing that carries an awkward ring to most Western ears. And in Ghana, you wouldn't request a truck so much as you would ask for a *lorry*.

At the moment, however, we want neither a truck nor a lorry, and the *Thank You Jesus* restaurant would be in no position to provide us with either. What I want is the jollof rice. I order it in English, but the waitress seems baffled.

"No chicken," she says hesitantly, her accent thick. "Spicy yes, spicy no."

I'm not sure exactly what she means, so I nod and smile. "Yes, spicy please."

The waitress is as black as my own mother. The restaurant is dimly lit, at least juxtaposed against the blinding sun that beats down on the pavement outside. Squinting through the window, I can make out a man with a large funnel on his head, which he appears to be wearing as a hat. He wanders out of my sightline to continue about his daily affairs, but soon afterwards, another man passes by who is equipped with what seems to be a flame thrower on his back.

Our jollof rice arrives, and it has chicken, which is *spicy yes*. Melody, who had requested the *spicy no* option, also receives *spicy yes*. We acknowledge that West Africa might be the only place that an Asian has ever declared there to be too much rice, but rice still has its uses. Here, that use is to soak up the flavourful spicy sauce in which the chicken has been submerged all morning.

We are relaxed. We've come this far without illness or injury, and Ghana is otherwise known as *Africa for beginners* – one driver promised that we could walk across *the whole of Ghana* and not encounter any problems. If this were the beginning of our journey, it would serve as a primer to low-level chaos, and like this jollof rice, it would be one spiced with a dash of good-natured Ghanaian charm. But instead, Ghana is the second to last stop, our eighth border crossing, with only the international airport in Togo still awaiting us.

When we leave the *Thank You Jesus* restaurant, we meet with concrete shacks abutting their wooden neighbours, constructed with boards nailed together at oblique angles. There are children scrubbing clothes in washbasins on the sidewalk. Teenagers sitting idle on concrete walls listening to hiplife music, and the bass of the boom boxes merges with the occasional hum of a passing tricycle. And in the gutters, there are goats bleating as they scrounge for morsels of food.

NO VISITOR TO CAPE COAST ESCAPES THE TOWN WITHOUT visiting its sordid castle. Melody, whose diet consists of museums and all things historical, has been anticipating this more than I have. For me, it is more difficult to imagine what a dead castle and a canned script could add to something I could peruse on Wikipedia for free.

The fortification itself is a glistening pearl pinned to the shores of the Atlantic. It shines alabaster white, its roof studded with black cannons that face the water, an impeccable white crown perched on the coast of Africa. Wooden boats and local fishermen dot the beaches below the turrets and rows of windows, enveloped in the haze of the crushing midday heat. Foaming waves sweep in from the ocean. It is a scene worthy of an oil painting, and I imagine it has been immortalized as such many times over.

A half dozen tourists comprise our group. Hiding at the rear is a Ghanaian couple with their child. At the fore is a solitary man who knows more about this castle and its history than any person could know by accident, and I wonder if he is a student historian. And finally, there are two black Americans who, from their accents, could be from the Deep South. That would make Cape Coast a pilgrimage of sorts, as culturally meaningful for African Americans as Mecca for Muslims, or Israel for the Jews.

The Portuguese stayed as colonizers for a hundred and fifty years. They were the architects of Elmina – a name which itself is a bastardization of the Portuguese word for *mine* – but their sights soon shifted from the gold trade to a more lucrative trade in humans. Indigenous Africans were captured and enslaved from all across the jungles of West Africa, brought to the castle in chains for hundreds of years. Sometimes, the Europeans would forcibly capture Africans, the barrel of a gun forcing their surrender. Other times, they would collaborate with a few complicit locals to raid villages and kidnap their prey. Sometimes the Africans themselves were deceived – promised better living conditions abroad or brought on board European ships as entertainment and then plied with alcohol.

But most often, we are told, they were prisoners of tribal wars who were captured by rival Africans, bartered to the Europeans, and then enslaved.

"They were stripped naked for every part of their body to be totally inspected," says our guide. "They branded them to show ownership, then moved them inside the dungeon to await shipment. They treated people like livestock."

The Dutch forcibly seized the castle from the Portuguese, before it finally became a British colonial possession late in the nineteenth century. It was only then that this brutal slave trade was abolished. At a glance, this development seems to be a reasonably positive contribution on the part of the British Empire, but unsurprisingly, our guide doesn't see it this way.

"This does not exonerate the British," he pointedly adds at the end of his scripted remarks.

By now, we are standing on the dried, matted, and petrified remains of what was once human waste. Once inside the slave castle, indigenous Africans waited in this damp, dimly lit dungeon anywhere from two weeks to three months, urinating and defecating amongst each other. If they became ill, they were transferred to a smaller dungeon where they were left to live or die. And die most of them did – from disease, long before they were ever shipped overseas.

There is a church built atop the dungeons, our guide tells us. *Heaven and hell*, as he describes it.

"The Europeans wanted to prove that their God was supreme. Just to prove that, they built a shrine on top many of the castles. *Hallelujah* was being sung up there, while we were dying down here."

We trail behind him in silence into a male prison cell for disobedient slaves. It amounts to nothing more sophisticated than a common torture chamber – here, the inmates would be deprived of such luxuries as food, water, and ventilation. It's pitch-black inside, even by the standards of the previous dungeons. The prisoners survived here for no more than seven days before they eventually suffocated. The desperate scratches of their chains still mark the wall. Nobody escaped alive.

"This is what will happen to you," says the guide.

The women were subjected to a different form of terror, one just as arbitrary, at the hands of the castle's governor.

"He gave orders to open the gate and they would assemble in the courtyard. The governor would select one woman of his own choice. Then they would open the reservoir so that she could wash. Then she would go upstairs where she would suffer rape."

Females who resisted their prescribed rape were chained to a cannonball or held indefinitely in a female punishment cell. If they accepted their role as concubine, inevitably some would become pregnant. After giving birth in town, they were brought back to the slave castle. Their mixed-race children were given European names and then raised by domestic slaves. Their European names prevented them from ever tracing their roots. When I hear this, I feel vaguely and irrationally self-conscious, since the history of mixed-race children hundreds of years ago has almost nothing to do with me.

Finally, we arrive before the door of no return. When our guide opens this heavy door, it is an ecstatic respite from the stifling heat and darkness of the dungeons. An ocean breeze wafts in from the water. Underneath the stone frame, the silhouette of our guide is backlit by the white midday sun, obscuring his features. The fishermen and the hustlers waiting outside see us emerge and begin to make their way towards us through the sand. The Ghanaian family on our tour poses for a grinning selfie portrait beside the door.

As we stand outside, our guide tells us that forty percent of these captured slaves were dispatched to Brazil, another forty percent to the Caribbean, and the remaining ten percent to the United States – mostly to work on the sugar plantations and replace indigenous labour. In sum, sixty million souls were stolen from West Africa, but a mere twelve million arrived at their final destination. In 1807, the trade was abolished. And with that, the tour suddenly ends.

Our guide remains, lingering awkwardly at the entrance to the museum, and so I press him further on who's to blame for these atrocities.

"Do you think that when the British realized what they were doing, and how abhorrent it was," I ask carefully, "that the entire practice just collapsed on itself?"

He doesn't hesitate for even a second before he explains that the British would never have abolished slavery based on any internal pressure within the Empire. The drive to abolish was entirely born within Africa, borne by Africans, and the British grudgingly relented from the enormous pressure to which they were subjected by Africans themselves.

"Slavery still exists like this," he tells me confidently. "It just takes different forms."

I nod and accept his explanation, because in the end, he is the expert, and I am not.

THE FOLLOWING DAY, WE FIND OURSELVES ON OUR WAY TO Esi's house, and it is already late in the afternoon. You wouldn't know it from the heat, which hasn't yet begun to dissipate, but you might suspect it from the length of the shadows trailing behind us.

It seems every building in Ghana bears at least one funeral poster, and sometimes as many as six. They are fascinating. Each is uniquely designed, emblazoned with the name, age, and photograph of the deceased, and each carries a detailed description of the upcoming funeral arrangements. Some of the posters simply call themselves obituaries, but more commonly they describe the death itself as a *Call to Glory*, a *Glorious Home Call*, a *Glorious Exit*, or a *Celebration of Life*. It would be easy enough to conclude that Ghana is obsessed with death, but it's not that straightforward.

In the West, we implicitly understand that ruminating about death is irrelevant (at least to the living) and therefore a waste of time. It's true that on some level, we recognize that those with whom we interact will all eventually die, but it is sufficient that for the time being, they have no immediate plans to do so. We rarely think about it, much less speak about it. But here in Ghana, it is all but impossible to escape a sense of both the importance of death and its omnipresent possibility. Its people relate to it with anticipation rather than dread, along with the acute awareness that it could befall them at any moment. Each generation nods to the next in a way that is both visible and unexpectedly joyous.

We pause in front of one of these posters, and moments later, a middle-aged woman's head pops out from her second storey window. I'm initially taken aback by her sudden attention, worried that reading a public obituary is somehow shameful, but the woman instead greets us with an unguarded smile.

"That is my mother," she declares to us.

She's eager to tell us all about her mother and explains

that the poster has been up for about two months. The woman in the windowsill looks no more than fifty, but the poster claims that her mother died at the ripe age of 120. She explains that her uncle, meanwhile, is only 95 years old. It seems like a stretch, but I'm not about to ask for their birth certificates.

"Can I take a picture?" I say instead. "Is it okay to take pictures?"

There's no hesitation. Yes. Of course.

"Do you mind if I ask you why there are...so many of these posters?" says Melody.

"In Ghana," says the woman in the windowsill, "we have two lives. To born, and to die. When you are born, you belong to the society. When you die, the whole of society come to mourn with you. All well-wishers are invited."

"And does everybody get one? A poster, I mean."

"Yes, of course," says the woman, and then immediately retracts her statement. "Maybe not if they are a bad man."

We continue onward down this sun beaten road, passing hand painted shop fronts and tattered umbrellas until we stop again next to another obituary. This one has been glued to a flat fence post, and then vigorously stapled on all sides for good measure. His is a *Glorious Home Call* at the more modest age of 102, and his photograph is black and white, faded and burnt by the sun, and followed by an impossibly lengthy list of his dozens of surviving children and grandchildren. I snap a picture with my phone.

A high-pitched whistle catches our attention, and we both turn to find a young man watching us from the schoolhouse across the street. He doesn't look pleased.

"No picture."

"Oh," I say, tucking the phone back into my pocket. I hesitate, and then cautiously approach him. "I didn't realize. People cannot take pictures of these?"

"No picture," he repeats, and he lifts his hand to his neck to give the impression of slashing his throat. "The man is dead."

But I assume that even Ghanaian people must take pictures sometimes, or else they would never remember where and when to arrive for the funeral services. I'm not sure if his objection is to what he presumes to be our morbid curiosity, whether it is based on superstition, or perhaps simply an implication that we are not part of his community – that we are tourists, and that taking pictures is a local privilege that we have not yet earned. With my light skin, I must represent the Europeans, and the Scramble for Africa that carved it up among the colonial powers. Melody represents the Chinese incursion, the Belt and Road initiative that trades infrastructure for political capital. Between us, all we know how to do is *take*.

But the woman in the windowsill seemed so happy.

Maybe the trouble with cultural generalizations is that people rarely agree on anything.

I think that if I were dead, I would want people to take my picture. I think that would be especially true if I went to the trouble of posting my picture publicly. It speaks to a sort of existential vanity that people's concept of death involves a primal fear of being forgotten by the living – and that living on somewhere inside a camera roll is still better than nothing.

ESI IS NOTHING SHORT OF STUNNING.

She has enormous afro hair highlighted with flecks of red, hoop earrings, and she wears a form fitting blue summer dress. She is beautiful, all in all. If she is not one of Charlie's Angels, then she must have stepped directly out of a Quentin Tarantino film and into this smoke-filled wooden hut. As we cook, tendrils of smoke drift lazily through the slats of wood and into the twilight air. The hot coals glow crimson, but when one falls from the stovetop, Esi picks it up with a bare, calloused hand and deposits it back into its proper place.

Outside, in the streets, the beat is hiplife. *Highlife music is for old people*, someone in Ghana told me, and hiplife is its natural evolution. In the bars, on the weekend, hiplife inevitably leads to an ecstatic and chaotic dance in which Ghanaians throw their arms in the air, vigorously whipping the towels they brought with them to wipe the sweat from their brows. But tonight, the locals merely sit curbside, content to listen and bathe in the unremitting heat.

For the moment, this hut is a cooking school. But it doubles as a restaurant, and triples as a sports bar, at least when the Liverpool/Westham game comes on television.

As the meal nears completion, the others arrive one by one. First, a girl who appears younger than her eighteen years arrives with two of her friends. She claims to be Esi's granddaughter, but since Esi couldn't be more than forty, I'm not sure how this could be true. She tells us that in Ghana, everyone learns to cook when they are six years old, whether male or female. She says that she can cook just as well as her grandmother, but doesn't say it with much confidence, so I don't believe her.

Esi pours more water, and then shows Melody how to fan the flames. The smoke is thicker now, a powerful and intoxicating scent. It's difficult to breathe. Minutes later, she removes the pot from the stove, again handling it with her bare hands. Her manner is confident and deliberate.

"Aren't you worried about burning your hands?" I ask her.

"It's hot, but I am used to it," says Esi.

Next, a middle-aged man arrives. He seats himself in a corner at the back of the hut, away from the smoke and closer to the television. After we introduce ourselves, he pours a clear concoction from a small bottle into two plastic tumblers and offers them to us. He calls it *apatesh*, the local moonshine. It is somehow even more potent than the *koutuku* that we were given in Côte D'Ivoire. It's fire in a bottle. It burns all the way down.

"Don't drink it on an empty stomach," he warns, only moments too late.

"Seems like every country has some sort of local drink like this," I say, feeling suddenly friendlier and somewhat dizzy. "But we don't have anything like this in Canada."

He scrutinizes me closely. "You say you are from Canada, but I can tell you are mixed race. I can see in your face that you might be from Ghana. Your nose, your cheeks."

"I can pass for most things," I answer, uncomfortable that he is making this personal. "Not Ghana, but you're right, my mother is from Trinidad. And my father came from England."

"They try to make you forget your roots. Maybe you are the first person in your family to come back to Africa.

"Yes, I think so." I attempt to change the topic. It occurs to me that I had assumed my family tree came to an abrupt end in St. Lucia, but I don't want to reveal the extent of my ignorance. "Where did the slaves come from? Did they only come from Ghana?"

"Not only Ghana. From West Africa, but they used Ghana as a main base. You been to the castle. I don't know how you feel. Stressed, sad."

At this point, Esi arrives at the table to deliver the products of our labour – a serving plate containing a stew of beans, palm oil and tomato paste called *red-red*, and another filled with a fiery mixture of spinach and ground chicken known as palava sauce. I'm hoping it will be an effective sponge for the *apatesh*.

"It's shocking," I say, truthfully. "It's shocking that we don't learn about it much in school, in history class. We spend time on the Second World War, on the Holocaust, but much less time on the slave trade."

"The Holocaust is nothing! The Holocaust is nothing. If you enter the castle at Elmina, you can feel that burden in the pit of your stomach."

"It's heavy stuff," I admit. He has piqued my interest. "It makes me wonder if my ancestors came from here."

"A lot of people in the Caribbean come from Ghana. They used to keep records. The last name, the tribe, and they know you are from a region. You can see the similarities in the food, the music, the dance. It's the same *genetic structure*."

It's true. You can hear it in the roots of Afro-Cuban music, in the drumbeats and the rhythm of rumba, in the movements of the dancers.

"They can use genetics to find out if you are Ashanti, or Fantse," he promises me. "You unnastand? You will have a lifelong identification with Africa."

IN ACCRA, THE STREETS OF JAMESTOWN ARE ALIVE AT SUN-
down. As we pass the Divine Game Centre, we see children
and teenagers play arcade games behind a drape. Outside,
others play checkers on the street. Still others play ping
pong. Only the foosball table sits idle. There is a peeling
sticker affixed to one side of the table.

NO GAMBLING

Melody has brought us to another slave fortress, this
one swallowed by the city centre and forgotten among the
thirty-eight similar castles scattered along the Gold Coast.
Abandoned, it has long since been reclaimed by the mass-
es – beggars in the courtyard, women sleeping among the
rubble and errant stones. Through one doorway, there are
men shouting in a foreign tongue as they pray. The courtyard has been transformed into an open-air classroom, and
on one side there are desks and a chalkboard in front of
a flight of steps that leads nowhere. We circumnavigate
the courtyard in the dying light of sunset, and then turn
back to the street, where vendors have turned on the single
lightbulb in each of their stalls to announce the arrival of
dusk.

Just down the road, there is a photography gallery, one
last landmark before we retreat to our hotel. Inside, the
single large room is filled with hundreds of black and white

photos of colonial Ghana, old presidents and historical figures from days when the only ones who would possess a
photograph of themselves were the wealthy and famous.
The room smells like an antique trunk in a stuffy attic.

A large man in traditional dress follows me through
the studio as I inspect the photos. He has intelligent eyes,
a wide face, and a powerful voice. He points out the anti-
colonial cultural heroes in a manner that makes me assume
that he must be the guide – but when I ask him directly, he
tell me he doesn't even work here.

"I just come around," he says. He reaches into a nearby
bookshelf, selects a prominent coffee table book and sets
it down next to us. "I am a historian of Black history and
I have written two books on this." As he flips through it,
each page contains an old black and white photo above,
and a block of explanatory text below. He returns to the
dustjacket, where his own picture is featured alongside a
short biography.

"My great grandfather was carried away from the Gulf
of Guinea. That is where we are now. I know the white man
very well. I took my time to school myself on the white
man while I obtained my law degree in London. And I have
returned so that my dust shall mingle with the dust of my
forefathers. This is what I want you to understand."

"I understand," I say, trying in vain to mirror his passion. He creates drama with every sentence that spills forth

from his mouth. But my own voice feels weak and trivial next to his. "My mother is from Trinidad, but I don't know anything about my family coming from Africa."

"You have African blood," he insists. "Read William Du Bois, Malcolm X – they are intellectually regarded as the fathers of Pan Africanism."

He seems to take it as a personal affront when I explain that I've never heard of the first man, and never read the work of the second.

"Yes," he badgers me. "You must read your revolutionaries, your Black authors. Learn your history. You cannot be that *flimsy* regarding your own self! I've always maintained you can never be any use to yourself if you cannot understand your own origins. Don't cheat yourself."

I'm uncomfortable with his constant use of the second person possessive. *Your revolutionaries. Your Black authors.* Aren't I as much the colonizer as the colonized?

"Okay, but how do the British react to all this?" I finally ask, gesturing across the room.

"They want to forget about it. The British don't want to talk about this again. They are so much ashamed because they were thieves. They have a type of…collective amnesia. What we easily forget about can happen again."

Collective amnesia. Collective responsibility. I stole, and I was robbed. I am both oppressor and victim. Or perhaps I am neither of those two equally unpleasant things.

"True," I mumble instead, and then, not knowing what else to say, I recycle yesterday's words. "We…we don't learn much about all this in school. They tell us about the Holocaust."

"The Holocaust was ten years." He pauses for effect. "Slavery lasted *three hundred years*!" he booms. Heads turn across the studio.

ANOTHER DAY, ANOTHER CASTLE. THIS TIME, OUR GUIDE IS young, but it's at first difficult to tell. He wears a trendy, buttoned up floral print shirt, but his face is hard, his cheekbones prominent, his eyes unusually intense.

"The Ghanaians see the beauty of this place," he muses. "They don't really listen to me. They want to take pictures, until you take them into the dungeon. We were not really taught about this in school in Ghana. You were told once and then you forget. So instead, they say: 'Let's go to the castle, it's beautiful.'"

"But those from the diaspora, a lot of them break down. The foreigners, people from the Caribbean, African Americans. They end up crying. They get here and understand what they went through. They say: 'This is family, this is history.'"

We continue through the castle, and he continues through his canned script of horrors. And then, maybe – just maybe – he goes off script. I can't be certain.

"The African raiders, one night as you are sleeping, they surround the village," he begins. "Then in the morning, they separate the rich ones from the poor ones."

"The chiefs sold *their own* people in tribal war. The Europeans only added trade to it. The Europeans saw the Africans were not united. So they said, why don't you bring them to me and you'll at least get something in return. And if the Dutch were giving more than the Portuguese, then the chiefs go to the Dutch."

"*We* made it a successful trade, not them," he continues. "I have American tourists who tell me, if the Africans had known, they wouldn't have done that. Don't tell me that. They would see them walking, in chains."

"One man on this tour, he wasn't ready to hear this. He says: 'You see a white man, you get angry. You see what the whites do to us. You should never mix with them.'"

"I say, don't get angry. We all play a role in this. I was trying to educate the man, but he wasn't ready to listen."

Lome,
Togo

REPUBLIQUE TOGOLAISE
D.G.D.N.-D
SERVICE DES VISAS ET DE L'IMMIGRATION

SAINTON
CHRISTOPHER JOHN

LE CHEF SERVIC

SIVAH
BEYELI SOSSO
Commissaire Prin
de POLIC

Printed in Great Britain
by Amazon